P-38 LIGHTNING VS Ki-61 TONY

New Guinea 1943–44

DONALD NIJBOER

First published in Great Britain in 2010 by Osprey Publishing,
Midland House, West Way, Botley, Oxford OX2 0PH, UK
44-02 23rd St, Suite 219, Long Island City, NY 11101
E-mail: info@ospreypublishing.com

A CIP catalogue record for this book is available from the British Library

ISBN: 978 1 84603 943 0
PDF e-book ISBN 978 1 84603 944 7

Edited by Tony Holmes
Cockpit, gunsight, three-view and armament artwork by Jim Laurier
Cover artworks and battlescene by Gareth Hector (P-38 model supplied by Milviz)
Page layout by Ken Vail Graphic Design, Cambridge, UK
Index by Alan Thatcher
Typeset in ITC Conduit and Adobe Garamond
Maps by Bounford.com
Originated by PDQ Digital Media Solutions, Suffolk, UK
Printed in China through Bookbuilders

10 11 12 13 14 15 10 9 8 7 6 5 4 3 2 1

P-38 Lightning cover art

On July 26, 1943 future 12-kill ace Capt James A. Watkins of the 49th Fighter Group's 9th Fighter Squadron almost made ace-in-a-day by shooting down a remarkable four Ki-61 "Tony" fighters over Markham Valley (in the eastern highlands of New Guinea). Ultimately the only Lightning pilot to down four Ki-61s in a single sortie, Watkins was flying his assigned aircraft, P-38G-10 42-12882, at the time. This artwork depicts the first of his four kills, which Watkins described in the following extract from his combat report. "I turned my flight into the attack at the rear after dropping belly tanks. Two inline aircraft ('Tonys') were coming down head-on. I shot at the first one and observed the canopy come off and the pilot jump out as the ship rolled over. The fighter was observed to catch fire, and this was confirmed by Lt Gerald Johnson, who was flying on my wing."
(Artwork by Gareth Hector)

Ki-61 "Tony" cover art

The primary users of the Ki-61 "Tony" in New Guinea were the Japanese Army Air Force's 68th and 78th Sentais, and their combat records were destroyed in-theater. How many P-38s were shot down by the Ki-61 and which pilot claimed the most are questions that will probably never be answered. The only thing that can be said for certain is that "Tony" pilots clashed with their counterparts flying the P-38 on numerous occasions over New Guinea, but they rarely emerged victorious. The aircraft seen on the cover of this volume is the Ki-61-Ia of Capt Shogo Takeuchi, who was assigned to the 2nd Chutai/68th Sentai. The latter was based at Wewak, New Guinea, in October 1943. Takeuchi was almost certainly the leading JAAF ace over New Guinea, having claimed 30+ victories (16 of them in the Ki-61 with the 68th) by the time he succumbed to wounds after clashing with P-47 Thunderbolts on December 15, 1943. Although no records exist detailing what aircraft Takeuchi shot down, he would have routinely clashed with P-38s acting as bomber escorts when he led his Chutai against USAAF B-24 heavy bombers sent to attack the Japanese stronghold of Wewak. One such clash took place on July 21, 1943 when Ki-61s from the 68th and 78th Sentais claimed five P-38s shot down for the loss of two "Tonys". The USAAF pilots were credited with three Ki-61s destroyed in return, without loss.
(Artwork by Gareth Hector)

CONTENTS

INTRODUCTION

OPPOSITE
A factory-fresh P-38F banks and climbs for altitude. When test flown against other frontline fighters – P-39D, P-40F, P-47C and P-51A – in March 1943, the USAAF concluded "The P-38F's best maneuver against all types tested was to climb rapidly out of range and then turn and commence the combat from a superior altitude. Once gaining this altitude it should retain it, making passes and climbing again rapidly. Knowledge of the local enemy fighter performance will dictate the tactics to be used by the P-38F in the combat zone. It is doubtful if this aircraft will meet in combat any type of enemy aircraft in which close-in fighting will be its best offensive action". (National Archives)

The P-38 Lightning was tailor made for the air war in the Pacific, but not by design. Fortunately, the Lockheed fighter entered service at the "right time" and at the "right place". It was a weapon well suited to its environment, and rarely in the history of warfare has an aircraft been better suited than the Lightning to the bitter conflict in the South Pacific. Thanks to this compatibility it soon became the weapon of choice for America's leading aces.

While the P-38's drawbacks hampered its performance as a long-range escort fighter in Europe, its service in the Pacific was second to none, making it one of the most successful interceptors of World War II. Lightnings from the Fifth and Thirteenth Air Forces savaged both the Japanese Army Air Force (JAAF) and Imperial Japanese Naval Air Force (IJNAF) in New Guinea and the Solomons. It was a remarkable accomplishment for an aircraft of such an unusual design that endured a troubled development and production program.

The P-38 proved itself to be a devastating fighter, and in March 1943 the United States Army Air Force (USAAF) considered the F-model to be "the best production line fighter tested to date. Types tested include the P-47C Thunderbolt, P-51A Mustang, P-40F Warhawk and P-39D-1 Airacobra".

The Lightning's nose armament of four 0.50-in. (12.7mm) machine guns and one 20mm cannon simply destroyed lightly built Japanese fighters and bombers. The first model of the Lightning sent to the Pacific in quantity was the P-38F, equipping the 39th Fighter Squadron (FS) of the 35th Fighter Group (FG). Capable of attaining a top speed of around 400mph, the Lightning was considerably faster than any Japanese fighter then in service, and its performance above 20,000 ft was exceptional. However, when compared to lighter and more maneuverable Japanese fighters, the Lightning was not a nimble aircraft. But when you consider its size and weight, the P-38 had a reasonably good turning radius, and it could turn inside a Mitsubishi A6M Zero-sen at high speed when at high altitude.

The Lightning's twin Allison V-1710 inline engines gave it an excellent rate-of-climb, and the propellers were set to turn in opposite direction so as to negate the torque that blighted single-engined fighters. The P-38's range was superior to other US fighters, but there was still room for improvement. When fitted with long-range drop tanks the Lightning had phenomenal range. Equipped with these qualities, the Lockheed fighter would see combat in an environment completely hostile to both man and machine.

The air war that was fought in the Southwest Pacific was unique. Surprisingly, there were no strategic targets that had any real value. There were no cities, or raw materials to be seized by either side. The key strategic importance of the area lay in its geographic value. The Southwest Pacific provided Japan with a "doorway" through which to project power and expand its defensive perimeter. It was one of the most hostile environments in which to fight, and one of the worst in World War II. It was one of the most primitive places on earth.

Everything required to fight had to be brought in from the outside. Airfield construction in the Southwest Pacific was based on trial and error. Almost nothing was known about the basic geography, and intense rainfall throughout the area of operations severely limited the available terrain on which to build airfields. To add to the misery disease was rife. This duly meant that pilots not only had to fight the enemy, but debilitating illnesses as well. Good air bases in the Southwest Pacific were critical for victory, and when one was found or captured it was considered a gift from the gods.

By the time the Kawasaki Ki-61 Hien, codenamed "Tony", entered combat in May 1943 with the JAAF, the Japanese Army viewed the strategic situation in the Southern Theater with some panic. Stripping units from Manchuria and China, the JAAF began moving aircraft to defend the Solomons. With just over 200 Ki-61 "Tonys" in service, it decided to deploy them all to Rabaul and New Guinea.

The Ki-61 was unique in two ways. Firstly, it was the only inline-engined Japanese fighter to see service in substantial numbers during World War II, and secondly, it was one of the rare cases where Germany and Japan collaborated technically. On many levels the Ki-61 clearly illustrated, better than any other Japanese aircraft, why Japan should have never entered into a war with the United States. From April to October of 1943, Kawasaki was producing just 50 aircraft a month – nowhere near the numbers required to keep units operational.

The Ki-61 was also notoriously unreliable and prone to engine failure. The lack of well-trained mechanics, a chronic shortage of spare parts and repair equipment and long supply lines only added to the Ki-61's sorry serviceability rates. By the time both the 68th and 78th Sentais (the first units equipped with the type, a Sentai was roughly equivalent to a USAAF fighter group in terms of its size) entered the theater American P-38 units were well established.

In July and August 1943, both the 68th and 78th Sentais set up their new headquarters at Wewak, on the northern coast of New Guinea. Their job was to provide air defence (which was almost impossible due to the lack of a well developed radar-assisted intercept system) for the nearby harbor and protect transport vessels sailing between Rabaul, on New Britain, and Wewak.

When operated correctly, the Ki-61 Hien was a very good fighter, being superior to the Zero-sen. It was reasonably fast – 368mph at 16,000ft – had a decent high altitude performance and could dive faster than the P-39 and all but match the P-40.

A large number of Ki-61-Ibs served with the Akeno Army Fighter School in Japan from early 1943 until war's end. A handful of the instructors at this unit had seen action with the aircraft in New Guinea. (via Philip Jarrett)

Captured Ki-61-Ia construction number 263 was extensively photographed in flight to help Allied pilots recognize the "Tony" when they met it in combat. First thought to be a license-built version of the German Bf 109E, gun camera results from New Guinea soon established that the Ki-61 was an all new inline-engined Japanese fighter. Remarkably, British aircraft recognition posters for the Southwest Pacific theater had drawings of both the Bf 109 and Fw 190 in Japanese service, the Messerschmitt fighter being given the Allied code name of "Mike" and the Focke-Wulf "Fred"! (National Archives)

The Ki-61 boasted armored protection too, which was previously unheard of in Japanese combat aircraft. It also had self-sealing tanks, which, although unreliable, were better than those in the Zero-sen or Ki-43.

The Kawasaki fighter's maximum range did not come anywhere near the A6M's, however, although with the Japanese now on the defensive range was not a critical factor. Like the majority of JAAF and IJNAF fighters of World War II, the Ki-61-Ia was lightly armed with just two 12.7mm and two 7.7mm machine guns. Adequate for fighter-versus-fighter engagements, these weapons were next to useless against heavy bombers – later variants were fitted with harder hitting 20mm cannon in place of the 7.7mm weapons.

Overall then, although the Ki-61 was a vast improvement on the Ki-43 and early versions of the A6M Zero-sen, it was still inferior to second-generation American fighters such as the F4U Corsair, P-38 Lightning and F6F Hellcat. The differences were slight, however, and in the hands of a good pilot the Hien would prove to be a deadly opponent.

CHRONOLOGY

1937

February US Army Air Corps (USAAC) challenges the American aircraft industry to submit designs for an experimental fighter with "the tactical mission of interception and attack of hostile aircraft at high altitude". Specifications call for a speed of 360mph (579kph) at altitude and a climb to 20,000ft (6,096m) within six minutes.

June 23 USAAC issues contract 9974, authorizing Lockheed to build one XP-38.

December Japanese Army instructs Nakajima to construct a fighter with retractable undercarriage, with a speed of 500kph and a range of 800km. It emerges as the Ki-43.

1938

December XP-38 is completed, disassembled and taken to March Field, California, during the early morning hours of New Year's Day 1939.

1939

January 27 First flight of XP-38.

February 11 XP-38 crashes on approach to Mitchel Field, New York.

April 27 An order for 13 service test YP-38s issued by the USAAC.

1940

January Kawasaki secures blueprints for the Daimler-Benz DB 601A engine, having received three examples.

February Japanese Army gives Kawasaki developmental contracts for Ki-60 heavy and Ki-61 light fighters.

May Britain and France order 667 Model 322s, which would later be named the Lightnings. By September USAAC orders totaled 673 aircraft.

September 16 First YP-38 takes flight. Speed 405mph (652kph) at 20,000ft.

1941

March Prototype Ki-60 starts testing. It is considered too heavy and dangerous, so focus turns to the Ki-61.

June 36 P-38Ds built and delivered.

August Japanese Army occupies southern Indochina. USA, Britain and the Netherlands ban oil exports to Japan.

October P-38E enters production, and over the next five months 210 are built.

December Prototype Ki-61 with license-built Ha-40 inline engine completed days before Japan commits itself to war against the US. On December 7 Japan attacks Pearl Harbor, Hawaii.

1942

April F-4 photo-recce version of P-38 begins operations from Australia.

The gleaming XP-38 prototype head on. The sharp, strong futuristic lines of Lockheed's new fighter are evident, the aircraft being a complete departure from the standard single-engined designs of the period. The XP-38 was also huge, weighing in at more than 15,000lbs and boasting a wingspan of 52ft. (National Archives)

Between December 1941 and July 1942, Kawasaki managed to produce just 12 experimental Ki-61s. Here, two of the prototypes (serials 6101 in the background and 6102 in the foreground) have their engines warmed up while a flight of JAAF Ki-49 heavy bombers fly overhead. The new prototypes were prone to accidents, resulting in the deaths of several experienced test pilots and a curbing in the JAAF's enthusiasm for the new fighter. (National Museum of the USAF)

April Delivery of 527 P-38Fs begins.

April 18 Early production Ki-61 intercepts a "Doolittle's Raiders" B-25 over Tokyo but cannot shoot it down. USAAC concludes that Japan is importing or producing Bf 109s.

August Kawasaki begins production of the Ki-61-Ia. By March 1943 131 have been built.

August 4 First Lightning victories are scored by P-38Es of the 54th FS when two Japanese flying boats are shot down near Umnak, in the Aleutians.

August 7 US forces land at Guadalcanal. USAAF forms Fifth Air Force in New Guinea.

November P-38Fs from 339th FS/347th FG are sent to reinforce air units on Guadalcanal.

November 18 Eight P-38Fs from 339th FS claim three Zero-sens shot down, these being the first victories scored by the Lightning in the South Pacific.

December 27 39th FS/35th FG (the first squadron to receive P-38Fs in the Fifth Air Force) scores its first victories (four) over a formation of "Vals", Zero-sens and "Oscars".

1943

January 9th FS/49th FG re-equips with the P-38G.

February 80th FS/8th FG trades its P-39Ds for P-38Gs.

April Ki-61-equipped 68th and 78th Sentais begin their move south towards the New Guinea theater.

April 18 16 P-38Gs of 339th FS intercept and down Adm Isoroku Yamamoto's G4M "Betty" transport over Bougainville.

July 18 39th FS encounters Ki-61 for first time and claims two destroyed.

July 19 Ki-61 pilots claim first two P-38s destroyed.

August Soon to be famous 475th FG declared operational with 431st, 432nd and 433rd FSs.

August Last of 601 P-38Hs delivered to the USAAF.

September First Ki-61-Ib built. Armament increased to four 12.7mm machine guns. Aircraft armed with two 12.7mm machine guns and two German-built 20mm Mauser cannon produced in parallel.

September 4 Australian troops land at Lae and Finschhafen, New Guinea.

1944

January Production of the up-gunned Ki-61-I KAIc commences.

January 9th and 39th FSs forced to relinquish their worn out P-38Hs for more plentiful P-47Ds.

February 17 Japan withdraws all active combat units from Rabaul. Concede South Pacific to Allies.

April 22 American 1st Corps land at Hollandia. 68th Sentai forced to evacuate. Wewak bypassed.

July 25 68th and 78th Sentais are disbanded. Many ground and aircrew join the infantry.

DESIGN AND DEVELOPMENT

P-38 LIGHTNING

The P-38 Lightning was one of America's most successful fighters of World War II. Indeed, it was the weapon of choice for ranking aces Majs Dick Bong (40 kills) and Tom McGuire (38 kills), but the road from the drawing board to combat operations was a long and unusual one.

As war clouds began to gather in Europe in the late 1930s, the USAAC and US Navy instigated programs to expedite the procurement of more modern combat aircraft types. Both services wanted new fighters and bombers, but the numbers ordered were initially small and production was slow. This would lead to development problems that ultimately affected later production for a number of aircraft.

In January 1937, the Lockheed Aircraft Corporation of Burbank, California, responded to the army's request for a new fighter. The USAAC's Circular Proposal Specification X-608 called for a high-altitude interceptor with "the tactical mission of interception and attack of hostile aircraft at high altitude". The specification also stated that the fighter had to have a maximum speed of 360mph at altitude and the ability to climb to 20,000ft within six minutes. The engine power available at the time caused many aircraft designers to state that the specification was unrealistic. The Lockheed design team led by Hall Hibbard and Clarence "Kelly" Johnston proposed a solution that was both unorthodox and brilliant at the same time.

Lockheed believed the only way to get the power required would be to use two engines combined with the new technology of turbo supercharging. A supercharger is simply a blower or air pump that shoves air into an engine. Its prime purpose is to enable the engine to produce power at high altitude. The higher an aircraft climbs the thinner the air, causing the engine to produce less power. There are two types of supercharger – the mechanically driven version that is coupled to the engine's crankshaft, and the turbo supercharger that utilizes all or a portion of the exhaust gas from the engine to power a turbine that drives the blower.

The USAAC first became interested in turbo supercharged engines in the 1920s and 30s. The superior performance its aircraft gained from using these powerplants was key to the concept of high altitude, long-range strategic bombing and, eventually, to the interception of enemy bombers also flying at high altitude. The externally fitted turbo superchargers of the B-17's Wright R-1820 Cyclones and the B-24's Pratt & Whitney R-1830 Twin Wasps produced smooth, reliable power at high altitude. However, when it came time to fit a turbo to a fighter engine it was a much tougher proposition. Traditionally, the single-seat piston-engined fighter had its single engine and cooling equipment in the forward section of the aircraft, with the pilot, auxiliary equipment and fuel behind it, leaving virtually no room for a bulky turbo unit.

In an attempt to solve this problem Curtiss initially produce the highly advanced, but mechanically unreliable, YP-37, with a turbo mounted on the side of the fuselage. This caused the pilot's compartment to be mounted nearly four feet further back on what was basically a P-36 airframe. The pilot's forward and downward views were severely limited as a result. The USAAC took delivery of 13 service test examples in 1939. The failure of this design, and Bell's innovative P-39 Airacobra with its side-mounted turbo (the fighter's airframe proved to be too small to accept the bulky turbo, which was ultimately dropped from production) and tricycle undercarriage, caused the USAAC to choose the single-stage, single-speed mechanically supercharged Allison V-1710 engine to power the P-39, P-40 and early P-51 Mustang.

Five YP-38s are seen here lined up on the Lockheed ramp at the company's Burbank, California, facility on November 17, 1941. While the XP-38 had been hand-built, the YP-38 was designed with efficient mass production firmly in mind. Armament was specified to be one M9 37mm cannon and two 0.50-in. and two 0.30-in. machine guns. It also had much larger radiators on the rear of the booms and completely redesigned engine nacelles that had the oil cooler air scoops repositioned beneath the propeller spinners. Service tests were flown by the 1st Pursuit Group at Selfridge Field, Michigan, in the spring of 1941. (National Archives)

The P-38 Lightning, however, was designed from the outset to be equipped with two-stage supercharging using turbos located in the twin booms behind each engine. But such a layout was not without its problems. While highly efficient, and with more flexibility as to where they could be located in an airframe, the turbos also required jet engine like high temperature materials. Early Lightnings had a lower gear ratio for the mechanical supercharger on the Allison V-1710-27/29 engines. This caused the turbos to work harder, and led to the disintegration of the turbine wheel due to over-speeding – blast shields were introduced on the inboard side of the turbos in order to protect the pilot from flying debris.

The problem that most plagued the P-38, however, was its inefficient supercharger intercoolers. The first Lightnings, from the early production models to the P-38H, used General Electric Type B turbos with intercoolers in-between. The latter were located on the leading edge of the outer wings. Output from the turbos ran through the wing's leading edge and back to the engine, channelling airflow through a separate space within the leading edge so as to cool the supercharged air. It was a clever design that never worked very well. As engine power increased and the turbos improved, the leading edge intercoolers were no longer up to the task, so with the introduction of the P-38J a completely new intercooler design was introduced. Housed in a new cowling below the front of each engine, intercoolers were placed beside the oil coolers.

While the H- and J-models shared the same V-1710-89/91 engines, the P-38H was limited to only 1,240hp at 27,000ft. For the P-38J, that figure rose to 1,425hp at 30,000ft because of the new intercooler design.

On June 23, 1937 the USAAC issued contract 9974, authorizing Lockheed to build one XP-38 prototype. The design elements the company incorporated into its new aircraft were very sophisticated, and some would say radical for the time. The result was an aeroplane 150 percent the size of a normal single-engined fighter. The twin-boom, twin-engined layout solved many problems associated with the ambitious Circular Proposal Specification X-608. The two large propeller discs greatly increased horsepower efficiency and the larger wingspan gave it better high altitude performance. Add the guns mounted on the centerline and the bonus of single engine return capability, and the P-38 was truly unique in the world of fighter aircraft. It was also the first fighter to exceed 400mph in level flight.

Construction of the XP-38 (USAAC serial number 37-457) began in July 1938 and it first flew on January 27, 1939. When the prototype left the production line it was a gleaming high tech wonder. Powered by two Allison V-1710-C series engines rated at 1,090hp, the XP-38 had tricycle landing gear, Fowler flaps for low speed handling, butt joints and flush riveting of the skin that spread the flight loads within the interior structure. Add a bubble canopy, metal-covered control surfaces and turbo supercharging and you had an aircraft that was years ahead of other contemporary fighter designs.

The first flight on January 27, 1939 was a success, and after five hours of total flying time the aircraft was scheduled for delivery to Wright Field, Ohio, on February 11. Taking off from March Field, California, test pilot Ben Kelsey headed east and landed at Wright Field, averaging 360 mph during the flight. Waiting for him was

Chief of the USAAC, Gen Henry H. "Hap" Arnold, who wanted the XP-38 flown immediately to Mitchel Field, New York, in order to generate some good press for the military. Kelsey duly obliged, but on his approach to Mitchel Field carburetor ice formed, causing a lack of power at a critical time. As he tried to ease in power the engines failed to respond and Kelsey struck the ground short of the runway. The aircraft was a total write-off.

Even with the crash the XP-38 had set a cross-continent speed record, thus helping Lockheed secure a contract for 13 service test YP-38s, dated April 27, 1939. The first of these machines did not fly until September 16, 1940, with the last one not being delivered until eight months later. Total P-38 production for 1941 amounted to just 196 aircraft, not one of which was fit for combat.

Many of the early problems afflicting the fighter were due directly to serious errors in management. The P-38 was a radical design that required the best designers and a large support team. An internal Lockheed report, written during the early years of the war, revealed that many of the company's best personnel were moved over to more lucrative export models like the Hudson light bomber, 200 of which were ordered by the British in June 1938. The report concluded that the large-scale delivery of the P-38 had been set back by about nine months because of bad management and elementary design failures. Even more damning was the conclusion that if Lockheed had concentrated its best people on the P-38 it would have been delivered sooner, and instead of Japanese A6M Zero-sens battling P-40s over Darwin in early 1942, they would have met the more formidable Lightning. But so great was the USAAC's need for a modern fighter, it had little choice but to wait.

With all World War II fighter designs, there were always trade-offs. Something had to be given up in order to achieve a desirable trait. In the case of the P-38 it was extremely vulnerable to compressibility – a problem that plagued all second-generation fighters. In combat, P-38 pilots had to be very careful when diving at high speed from

A well-weathered P-322 runs up its engines ready for a training flight from Williams Field, Arizona, in 1943. Three years earlier, before the fall of France, the French had ordered 417 P-38s, designated as P-322-Fs, and the British had acquired 250 as P-322-Bs. Subsequently named the Lightning I, only three were delivered to the RAF and none to the French. These Lightnings had no turbo superchargers and the propellers were not counter-rotating. As a consequence their performance was quite poor and the British refused further deliveries. The remaining 140 Lightning Is were completed by Lockheed, modified to American standards and designated P-322s – P for pursuit and 322 for the Lockheed model designation number. All were used as trainers or in various experimental roles. (National Archives)

high altitude. If not, the aircraft's velocity would build up very quickly, causing its nose to tuck under and the dive to steepen, locking the controls. This left the pilot with little option but to bail out (if possible), or to "ride" the aircraft until it reached denser air, where he might have a chance to pull out.

Remarkably, it was not until October 1942 that a full-scale model of the P-38 was accepted for high-speed wind tunnel tests at the National Advisory Committee for Aeronautics' Ames Laboratory, in California. This was perhaps the single most significant lapse in the Lightning's development, as the problem had first appeared during YP-38 trials in May 1941. The solution to the P-38's compressibility woes was to fit dive brakes under each wing outboard of the engines, but these did not appear until the last batch of P-38Js rolled down the Burbank production line in June 1944.

Despite the compressibility problem, the USAAC pressed ahead with the fighter. Twenty-nine would be delivered as P-38s, with the same V-1710-27/29 engines as the YP-38, but the armament changed to one 37mm Oldsmobile cannon and four Browning M-2 0.50-in. machine guns. These aircraft were followed by 36 improved P-38Ds. Combat reports from Europe in the spring and early summer of 1941 demonstrated that the P-38 was not ready for action in its present form. Combat Command and Air Material Command therefore decreed that all aircraft in production had to have certain items in order to make them frontline capable. This included self-sealing fuel tanks, improved armor plate, a low-pressure oxygen system and bulletproof front windscreen.

The P-38D was the first step in making the new fighter combat ready. While changes had been made to improve both its operational effectiveness and serviceability, the D-model was still not deemed to be up to European standards by the USAAF, and only 66 examples were produced. For a brief period, the USAAF considered naming the P-38 "Atlanta", but fortunately adopted the British name of Lightning instead. (National Archives)

No B- or C-model aircraft were produced, Lockheed choosing instead to install the combat modifications and upgrades into the P-38D. This variant proved to be a fast fighter, with a top speed of 390mph at 25,000ft. However, even with the new "combat" modifications the D-model still came up short when compared to its European counterparts in terms of mission survivability. In response the D-model was redesignated the RP-38D in 1942, the "R" prefix meaning "restricted to non-combat roles". All RP-38Ds would be used as training aircraft instead.

Next to roll off the production line was the P-38E, 210 of which were built and delivered between October 1941 and February 1942. Armament was again changed

A factory-fresh P-38E sits at Hammer Field, in Fresno, California, on 4 March 1942. With the E-model the 37mm cannon was replaced by a license-built Hispano 20mm weapon, with 150 rounds, and the Hamilton Standard Hydromatic propellers with hollow steel blades were swapped for Curtiss Electric propellers with dural blades. The fighter was also painted with the standard Dark Olive Drab and Neutral Sea Gray camouflage according to Technical Order No 07-1-1. (National Archives)

to one 20mm Hispano cannon and four 0.50-in. machine guns. This would be the first version to see combat in World War II when, in April 1942, P-38Es were rushed to the Aleutians to equip the 54th FS.

The E-model was quickly followed by the much improved P-38F, which was considered to be the first truly combat-ready version of the Lightning. Powered by two 1,225hp turbo supercharged Allison V-1710-49/53 engines, it had a top speed of 395mph at 25,000ft.

The F-model differed from the P-38E in two distinct areas. Firstly, maximum weight was up to 18,000lbs (versus 15,482 lbs for the E-model) due to the fitment of extra protective armor, and this meant more powerful engines had to be used but internal fuel capacity was decreased. The latter was addressed with the development of underwing pylons capable of carrying drop tanks or bombs. Now the P-38 could carry two 165US gal drop tanks or two 1000lb bombs. Secondly, the F-model was fitted with "combat flaps". This was a modification made to the flap actuators that allowed the flaps to be deployed to a maximum angle of eight degrees during combat. The increased lift when using the flaps made the aircraft more maneuverable.

As the only genuine high altitude fighter in the USAAF's inventory, the P-38F had begun to see large-scale action in North Africa, New Guinea and the Solomons by late 1942.

The P-38F was quickly followed by the G- and H-models. The former was essentially the same as the F except for new engines (V-1710-51/55s, developing 1,325hp each) and revised radio equipment. The P-38H also had increased horsepower thanks to the installation of two Allison V-1710-89/91 engines rated at 1,425hp each, and the aircraft also featured automatic oil radiator grilles for improved cooling and the first fully automatic supercharger controls. Top speed reached 402mph at 25,000ft. As the war in the southwest Pacific gained momentum, it would be these three versions that would take the fight to the enemy, and in the end play a major role in the destruction of both the JAAF and the IJNAF in this theater.

The last two versions of the Lightning to see combat would be the P-38J and L, which were easily recognizable by the deep intakes beneath their propeller spinners

P-38J-15 LIGHTNING
37ft 10in.
UNCLE
Angel
9ft 10in.
52ft 0in.

that housed a completely new intercooler design. While the H- and J-models shared the same engines, the latter, with the new intercooler, could obtain 1,475hp at 30,000ft compared to the P-38H's 1,240hp at 27,000ft. With the intercooler radiators now located between the oil coolers, and not in the wings, the new J-model was fitted with 55US gal fuel tanks in their place. The P-38J/L would also incorporate all that had been learned up to this point with the aircraft in combat, thus making them the most potent Lockheed fighters of them all. In the case of the J-model, 2,970 were produced.

Speed was increased to 414mph at 25,000ft, but it was not until the last 210 of these machines came off the assembly line in June 1944 that they realized their full combat potential, as these airframes were fully equipped with dive brakes, aileron boost, improved cockpit heating and electrical system circuit breakers.

Embodying all of these improvements from the start, the P-38L was the ultimate Lightning, and the one equipped with the most powerful engines in the form of two Allison V-1710-111/113s rated at 1,600hp at 28,700ft. This advantage was somewhat negated by the extra 500lb of weight that was added to the airframe through various combat upgrades, however. One of the most unique features of the P-38L was the installation of new tail-warning radar. This compact transmitter receiver system picked up the presence of an aircraft in a cone behind the Lightning and immediately warned the pilot by an audible warning bell and a flashing red light beside the gunsight.

Ironically, the new P-38L was looked upon rather indifferently by veteran pilots in the Pacific. They viewed the power-assisted ailerons and dive flaps as a luxury rather than a necessity. Young pilots had to be cautioned not to use them in the belief they might be able to dogfight with a Japanese fighter. In the case of the flaps, fitted principally to eradicate the compressibility problems, they were hardly ever used, for most of the combats involving the P-38 occurred at or below 15,000ft. The P-38L was built in the greatest numbers, with 3,810 being produced.

When all the pluses and minuses were added up in respect to the Lightning in the Pacific, four factors stood out that all fighter pilots would agree – the aircraft possessed excellent speed, phenomenal range, devastating firepower and spectacular performance in a climb.

OPPOSITE
This aircraft, whose serial is unknown, was assigned to Capt Cy Homer of the 80th FS/ 8th FG in early March 1944. Flying from Nadzab, in northeastern New Guinea, Homer enjoyed great success with it during the early spring over Hollandia. He claimed a "Tony" destroyed and two more damaged on March 30, followed by the destruction of two "Oscars" and two "Tonys" on April 3. These victories took Homer's tally to 13, and he would claim his 14th kill (another Ki-43) on July 27. Homer's nickname within the 80th FS was "Uncle Cy", hence the titling applied to the fighter's nose. The green and white checks painted onto the P-38's rudders were unique to this aircraft.

Ki-61 HIEN (SWALLOW)

The JAAF's newest fighter when the Pacific War commenced was the Nakajima Ki-43 "Oscar". Like the Mitsubishi A6M Zero-sen, it adhered to the low-weight/high-maneuverability formula, but was not as good overall as the IJNAF fighter. Weighing almost 800lbs less than the Zero-sen, the Ki-43 was one of lightest single-engined monoplane fighters of the war. Powered by the same Sakae radial engine as the Mitsubishi, the Ki-43 was the most nimble fighter of World War II, superior even to the Zero-sen. And when circumstances favored its pilot, the "Oscar" was a dangerous opponent. But the JAAF's fighter units paid a high price for their aircraft's only positive attribute.

Like their Japanese counterparts, the Americans had an extremely hard time keeping captured Ki-61-Ia construction number 263 serviceable. Maintenance and safety issues were a priority, and on July 2, 1945 – little more than a month after its first flight in the US – the aircraft was written off in a belly landing at Yanceyville, North Carolina, after it suffered an in-flight engine failure. The Hien was en route to Eglin Field, Florida, from NAS Patuxent River, Maryland, at the time of the accident. (National Archives)

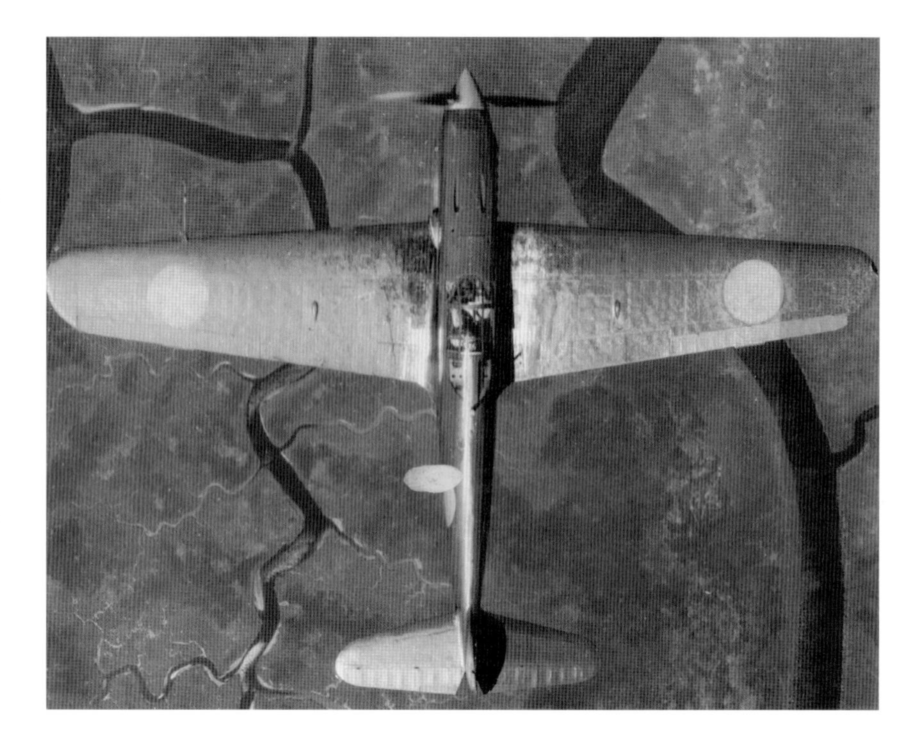

Design wise the Ki-43 was no match for the Zero-sen, and as a consequence it was 40mph slower. The aircraft was also appreciably slower than all US fighters. Originally armed with just two 7.7mm machine guns, the "Oscar" was later up gunned to two 13mm weapons, but this was still pitifully inadequate. Like the A6M, the Ki-43 had no armor or self-sealing tanks, and its airframe was even less durable than its naval counterpart. Some Allied pilots called it "a performing fool".

In fairness to the JAAF, it soon realized that the Ki-43 was not up to the task when compared to more modern American and British designs, and it quickly began to develop entirely new models of fighter. The first to emerge were the Kawasaki Ki-60 and Ki-61.

The latter machine was unique for two reasons. Firstly, it was the only inline Japanese fighter to see combat service. Secondly, it was one of the rare cases of technical cooperation between the Germans and Japanese in World War II. During the interwar period Kawasaki had cultivated a good relationship with Daimler-Benz, and in early 1940 it secured blueprints for the company's DB 601A (1,150hp) engine as fitted to the Luftwaffe's most advanced fighter, the Bf 109E. The DB 601A featured a single-stage supercharger that gave the Messerschmitt good performance above 30,000ft. Along with the blueprints, the Germans shipped three complete engines to serve as production patterns. Messerschmitt also played its part by delivering two Bf 109Es by submarine for the Japanese to test and evaluate. The adaptation of the DB 601 engine to Japanese production techniques began immediately, and the first Japanese-built version, designated the Ha-40 by Kawasaki, was completed in July 1941.

The JAAF had given Kawasaki developmental contracts for two new interceptors – the Ki-60 heavy and Ki-61 light fighters – in February of the previous year.

By March 1941 the Ki-60 prototype was ready for flight, this aircraft being a clean, all-metal stressed skin monoplane that was heavily armed with two 20mm Mauser MG 151 cannon and two 12.7mm machine guns. Due to its high wing loading (which made it laterally unstable and excessively heavy on the flight controls), high stalling speed and inferior take-off and landing performance, the Ki-60 was deemed unsuitable for further development. Even before the prototype's first flight, the JAAF had shifted its focus to the companion Ki-61.

Like the P-38, the Ki-61 Hien was plagued by a long development period and low production numbers (only 34 were built in 1942). By December 1941 the first prototype was ready for flight-testing. Ironically, the first Ki-61 was bigger and heavier than the Ki-60, despite it ostensibly being the light fighter variant. Unlike the Ki-60, the Ki-61 was fast, attaining a top speed of 367mph – compared to the Ki-60's 348mph – in tests at Kagamigahara airfield in early 1942. The JAAF ordered three experimental aircraft and nine additional test models. Twelve test aircraft had been completed by August 1942, and the first example built using production tooling rolled off the assembly line shortly afterwards.

Following handling and performance tests, during which a maximum speed of 367mph was reached, service trials began. Compared to the Ki-43 and A6M Zero-sen, the Ki-61's wing loading was very high – this drew stinging criticism from JAAF pilots. But for the majority who flew the new fighter, they were impressed by its high diving speeds, armor protection, self-sealing fuel tanks and improved armament. When test flown against the P-40E, Bf 109E, Ki-43-II and Ki-44-I, the Ki-61 was deemed to have the best performance overall.

Although the Ki-61 suffered from a number of unexplained accidents and engine failures during the flight test phase, the aircraft was accepted for service use under the designation Army Type 3 Fighter Model Ia Ko when armed with two fuselage-mounted Type 1 12.7mm machine guns and two wing-mounted Type 89 7.7mm machine guns, and Model Ib Otsu when armed with four 12.7mm guns. In August 1943 the wing guns of 388 Ki-61-Ia/bs were replaced by imported Mauser MG 151 20mm cannon. This made the Ki-61 the most heavily armed single-seat fighter in the

This Ki-61-I also belonged to the Akeno Army Fighter School. The first Hien flying school, it was responsible for training pilots assigned to the 68th and 78th Sentais prior to the units' posting to New Guinea in the spring of 1943. A small teardrop bulge can be seen on the uppersurface of the left wing just above the main gear landing strut. This accommodated the Type 89 7.7mm machine gun. The school had about 50 fighters on strength, and most, if not all, were unpainted with a bare metal finish. (National Museum of the USAF)

OPPOSITE
This aircraft was reportedly flown by Capt Shogo Takeuchi, leader of the 68th Sentai's 2nd Chutai, from Wewak, New Guinea, in October 1943. Historians credit Takeuchi with more than 16 enemy aircraft shot down over New Guinea and 30+ destroyed or damaged in total while flying in both the China-Burma-India Theater and New Guinea. Just how many victories he claimed in this particular aircraft remains unknown. The fighter is adorned with a chutai leader's white fuselage band, edged in red, as well as the 68th Sentai's distinctive tail marking. The latter was applied in white on 1st Chutai machines and in yellow on 3rd Chutai aircraft.

Pacific on either side. As the supply of MG 151s ran out and a comparable cannon of indigenous design was unavailable, the Ki-61 reverted back to four 12.7mm machine guns.

By February 1943 initial deliveries of the Ki-61-I had been completed, and the 23rd Dokuritsu Dai Shijugo Chutai at Ota began pilot conversion and training. Production-standard Ki-61s first saw combat with the 68th and 78th Sentais over the north coast of New Guinea, and operations soon revealed the fighter to be seriously flawed. Engine and main bearing failures and oil system faults were common, while a lack of spare parts and well-trained mechanics greatly reduced the type's serviceability. Even when the Ki-61s started to be delivered in larger numbers, a very high percentage failed inspection and had to be repaired before they left Japan. Servicing equipment was also in short supply, or nonexistent, and the closest Ki-61 supply depot to New Guinea was 1,000 miles away. Engine changes could not be made in the field, so complete aircraft had to be shipped to Clark Field, near Manila in the Philippines.

In an effort to address these issues, Kawasaki decided to simplify and strengthen the Hien's structure for the next version. With the indigenous Ho-5 20mm cannon now available in good numbers, the Ki-61-I KAIc (KAI standing for "kaizo", or modified) was produced. The new fighter was 7.5-in. longer and featured a detachable rear section, fixed tail wheel, stronger wings and wing attachment points for two 550-lb bombs or drop tanks.

For all its faults, the Ki-61 was well liked by it pilots. All versions handled well, and while not as maneuverable as the Ki-43, it was well respected by Allied pilots. And now for the first time JAAF pilots could dive away from trouble without the fear of their aircraft breaking apart. The added armor and self-sealing fuel tanks made the Hien pilots a more aggressive group when compared to their Ki-43 brethren. Armament now consisted of two Ho-5 20mm cannon mounted on the upper fuselage, with two 12.7mm guns in the wings. Production of the Ki-61-I KAIc began in January 1944, completely supplanting earlier versions on the production line.

This captured Ki-61-I KAId of the 19th Sentai was photographed at Clark Field, in the Philippines, in April 1945. After the IJNAF lost the Battle of the Philippine Sea in June 1944, it became apparent that America's next target would be the Philippines itself. In preparation, the JAAF sent the 17th and 19th Sentais, equipped with Ki-61s, to Neilson field, Manila, in mid-June. The white lines on the aircraft were applied by the USAAF for measurement and data collection purposes. (National Archives)

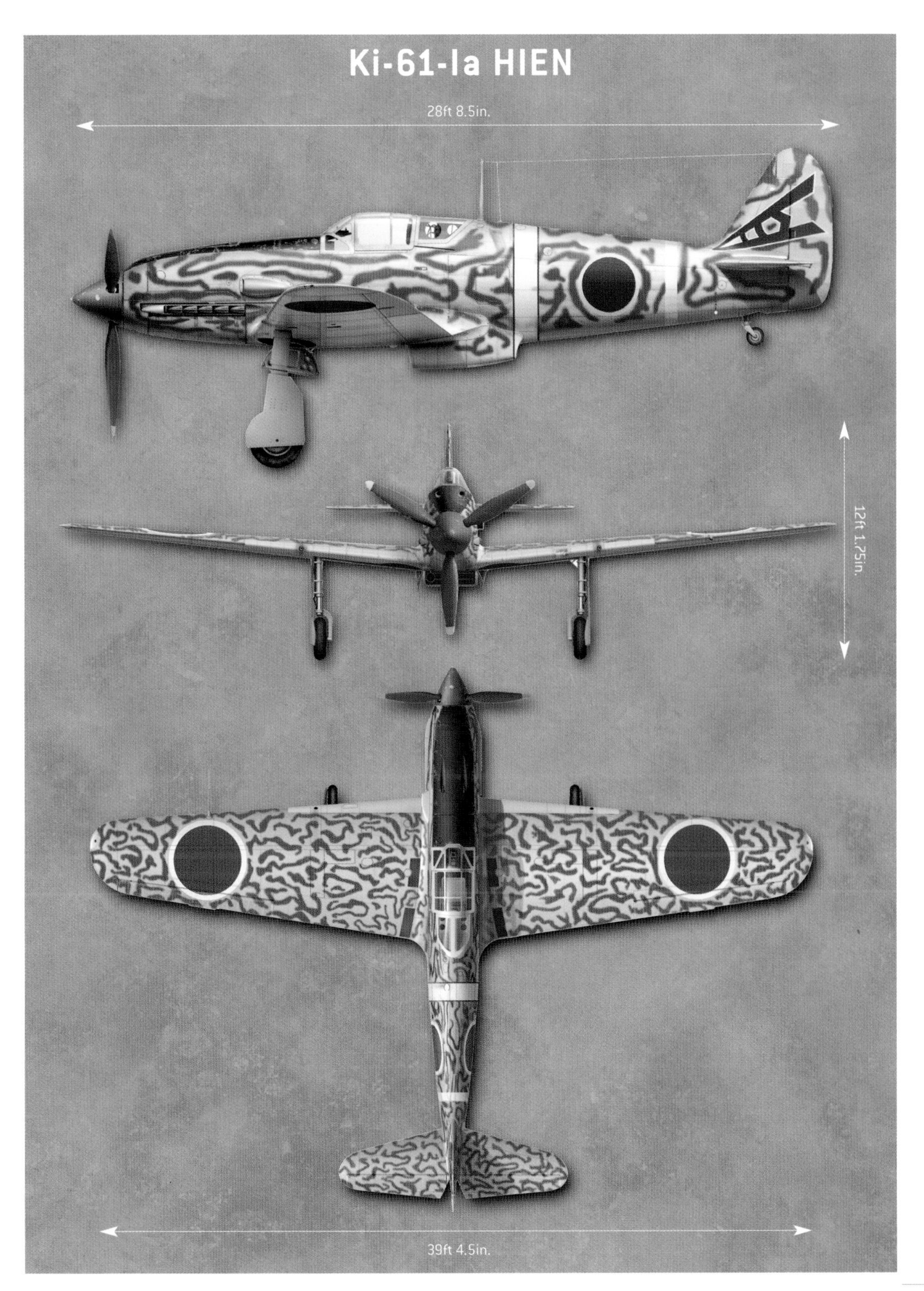
Ki-61-Ia HIEN
28ft 8.5in.
12ft 1.75in.
39ft 4.5in.

The perfect shot. Like most World War II fighters, the view for the pilot both behind and below was severely restricted in the Ki-61. American pilots considered the side and rear vision from the Hien to be "fair", and its cockpit layout was found to be good, although small, and for the Southwest Pacific theater very hot. (National Archives)

While monthly production of the Ki-61 reached a peak of 254 in July 1944, it was still miniscule when compared to the vast output of Allied fighters.

A few Ki-61-I KAId bomber interceptors were also produced in late 1944, these aircraft being heavily armed with two 12.7mm guns in the fuselage and a pair of Ho-105 30mm cannon in the wings.

The final version of the Hien family was the Ki-61-II, development of which commenced in the autumn of 1942. Powered by the uprated Ha-140 engine, which developed 1,500hp, the first specially redesigned Ki-61 was completed in December 1943. The prototype had a wing area increased by ten percent and a redesigned aft canopy for improved pilot visibility, but flight trials were blighted by poor engine reliability – the Ha-140's crankshaft proved to be particularly weak. Structurally, the revised airframe was unable to cope with the additional power produced by the engine, resulting in the wings cracking in flight. After production of just eight aircraft, the ninth airframe was modified as the Ki-61-II KAI. Production of this new variant commenced in September 1944, with two versions initially being built – the model IIA, with an armament of two fuselage-mounted 20mm Ho-5 cannon and two wing-mounted 12.7mm machine guns, and the IIB, armed with four 20mm Ho-5 cannon.

Only a handful of Ki-61-IIs ever saw combat. When its engine was operating correctly, the aircraft was an effective interceptor. Indeed, it was the only JAAF fighter capable of taking on the B-29 Superfortress at high altitude. Finally, on January 19, 1945 USAAF bombers destroyed the Akashi engine plant, ending the supply of Ha-150 engines. Of the 374 Ki-61-II KAIs built, 30 were destroyed on the ground prior to delivery and 275 were left languishing without powerplants at Kawasaki's Kagamigahara factory. Providing the latter machines with a suitable engine gave birth to one of the finest fighters of World War II – the Ki-100.

Utilizing the remaining 275 Ki-61-II airframes, Japanese engineers hastily installed the Mitsubishi Ha-112-II water-methanol injected radial engine with remarkable results. The new powerplant was almost twice as wide as the existing Ki-61 fuselage, which meant that an entirely new engine mount had to be produced. Using an Fw 190A-5 that had originally been sent to Japan in 1943 as a template, the engineers initiated a crash program based on the Focke-Wulf's engine mount. Four airframes were produced – one prototype, two experimental aircraft and one production machine. Between February and August 1945, Kawasaki was able to produce 378 Ki-100s, which in turn equipped four fighter regiments. Rated by many to be Japan's premier piston-engined fighter, the Ki-100 saw considerable action during the ill-fated defense of the Japanese Home Islands.

TECHNICAL SPECIFICATIONS

P-38 LIGHTNING

P-38

This was the first production variant to be ordered and built, with 30 examples being delivered to the USAAC in June/July 1941. The aircraft had limited armor protection for the pilot, and its armament consisted of four 0.50-in. machine guns and one M9 37mm cannon (the YP-38 had been armed with two 0.50-in. and two 0.30-in. machine guns and a 37mm Oldsmobile M9 cannon). Armor plate was added around the cockpit, along with a bulletproof windscreen. Power was provided by two turbo supercharged Allison V-1710-27/29 engines rated at 1,150hp. All examples were delivered in Olive Drab and Neutral Gray camouflage. Top speed was 395mph at 20,000ft.

P-38D

Priority reports coming from the Royal Air Force (RAF) gave a clear indication of what was required in order to make the P-38 a real fighting machine. US fighters with a "D" suffix denoted that they had been brought up to European combat standards. Self-sealing tanks were installed for the first time, but maximum fuel capacity was reduced from 410US gal to 300US gal. The high-pressure oxygen system was replaced by a new low-pressure one, more armor was added, new propellers were installed, along with a retractable landing light, and new elevator mass balances were put in place. Armament and powerplants remained the same as for the P-38. All 36 D-models were delivered by the end of August 1941, and along with the P-38s, they were issued to US-based training units as RP-38s and RP-38Ds.

P-38E

The E-model was the first major production version to come off the assembly lines, although it was only considered to be an interim version before the completion of the P-38G. The P-38E was a major step forward in the development of the Lightning. More than 2,000 modifications were made to the airframe between the D and E versions. Many were minor, but one of the major changes was in armament, where an Hispano M1 20mm cannon replaced the 37mm gun. This gave the Lightning a faster rate of fire, carried more ammunition (150 rounds) and was considered more effective in combat than the heavier 37mm gun.

The E-model was also the first version to be produced on a planned and effective assembly line, which meant the latest modifications could be added while the aircraft were still being built. Engine power remained the same as for the D-model, as did the maximum speed. Of the 210 produced, a number were set aside for testing, and 99 were converted into F-4-1-LO unarmed, high speed photo-reconnaissance aircraft.

P-38F

A total of 526 P-38Fs were produced, this number including 150 P-322-B Lightning Is intended for the RAF. Because the American government would not allow the export of turbo supercharger technology, the British aircraft did not have this equipment installed, and the aircraft suffered accordingly – particularly above 12,000ft. The RAF pilots that test flew the aircraft in California were not impressed, and only three were ever accepted (and just one made it to the UK). The rest of the order was uprated by Lockheed to F-model standards through the fitment of the turbo supercharger and issued to the USAAF.

The armament for the P-38F remained the same as for the E-model, and all subsequent versions of the Lightning would also boast four nose-mounted 0.50-in. machine guns and one 20mm cannon. Engine power was upgraded, however, with two Allison V-1710-49/53s developing 1,325hp. The P-38F was also the first Lightning to carry drop tanks in the form of two 165US gal tanks carried between the fuselage pod and the engines. The F-model was considered to be the first truly combat worthy version of the Lockheed fighter, and production examples began rolling off the Burbank line in February 1942.

In March 1943 the P-38F was test flown against the P-39, P-40, P-47 and P-51. A portion of the report titled "Tactical Suitability of the P-38F type Airplane" appears below:

> Maneuverability – The subject aircraft was flown in mock combat against P-39D, P-40F, P-47C-1 and P-51A types of aircraft, and the following results were obtained:

A P-38F undertakes a training mission over snow-capped mountains in 1942. The new F-model now weighed more than 19,000lbs, but its engine power had been increased to offset this. Internal fuel capacity was reduced, however, and this in turn led to the development of underwing pylons capable of carrying bombs or drop tanks. With two 165US gal tanks, the P-38F had a range of approximately 1,000 miles. (National Archives)

The subject aircraft could out climb all other types used in the test. The P-47C-1 was faster at all altitudes, and the P-40F and P-51A were faster up to 15,000ft. The P-39D was considerably slower.

Against the P-39D, P-51A and the P-40F, the P-38F had a longer radius of turn below 12,000ft. From 12,000ft to approximately 15,000ft, the radius was almost the same, and from 15,000ft on up, the P-38F had an equal or shorter radius of turn. In the initial turn, due to the slowness of aileron roll of the P-38F, the other types could roll into a turn faster and close up the circle rapidly before the P-38F would reach its maximum radius of turn. It would then take the P-38F sometime, if ever, to overcome this initial disadvantage.

The P-38F's best maneuver against all types tested was to climb rapidly out of range and then turn and commence the combat from a superior altitude. Once gaining this altitude it should retain it, making passes and climbing again rapidly. Knowledge of the local enemy fighter performance will dictate the tactics to be used by the P-38F in the combat zone. It is doubtful if this aircraft will meet in combat any type of enemy aircraft in which close-in fighting will be its best offensive action.

Ceiling – The operational ceiling was approximately 30,000ft and the service ceiling approximately 38,000ft, due to engine coolant and carburetor air temperatures becoming excessive.

Cockpit Arrangement – The cockpit is crowded and the switches and controls are arranged in a disorderly fashion. This is due in part to the large offset control column and the wheel which prevents the right side of the cockpit from being used for any control handles or switches. This large control column also hides the switch panel at the bottom of the instrument panel. The oil cooler control switches are too hard to reach for switches that have to be used numerous times during flight, and they require the pilot to keep his head in the cockpit during the time the oil shutters are changing positions (automatic coolers are recommended). The trim controls are separated widely in the cockpit. An ideal arrangement of trim controls may be seen in a P-51A.

In temperate weather the cockpit at lower altitudes is warm enough, but in climbing to altitude the cockpit becomes very cold, and remains that way. This will require pilots flying in tropical climates to wear heavy flying clothes when going on normal missions that may require altitude flying.

Visibility – The visibility over the nose is satisfactory for deflection shooting, but the armor plate window and gunsight obstruct the forward vision for search. To the sides the view downward is limited definitely by the position of the wings and engine, and searching below will have to be accomplished by banking the aeroplane from side to side. The search view on both sides is greatly obstructed by metal strips where the canopy joins the window. The view to the rear is limited by the boom and rudders, and rear armor plate.

A slightly stepped down position will be required for formation flying due to the position of the engines. A looser formation will be required than for single-engined fighters due to the two engines and to lag, and the overspeeding of the turbos."

P-38G

Generally similar to the F-series, the new G-model had numerous improvements, including winterization equipment that would be more useful in the Aleutians than New Guinea. The first P-38G rolled off the production line in June 1942, this variant being powered by Allison V-1710-51/55 engines that had increased boost ratings offering 1,325hp for take-off, but limited to 1,150hp at 27,000ft due to inadequate cooling. Lighter than the F-model by some 200lbs, the P-38G would be the most widely built example of the early Lightning variants – 1,082 had been delivered by March 1943, with a further 181 completed as photo-reconnaissance F-5As. The P-38G's maximum speed was 345mph at 5,000ft, 360mph at 10,000ft and 400mph at 25,000ft. It had a range of 850 miles on internal fuel at a cruising speed of 219mph at 10,000ft.

The first P-38G rolled off the Burbank production line in June 1942. Differences between it and the preceding F-model were slight, the G being equipped with the Allison V-1710-51/55 engine with increased boost ratings that offered 1,325hp for take-off. Due to inadequate cooling the new engines were limited to 1,150 hp at 27,000 ft, however. (National Museum of the USAF)

P-38s were hard to come by in the Southwest Pacific, with both the Fifth and Thirteenth Air Forces having to make do with a limited supply. Maintenance was a high priority, as units struggled to keep their dwindling number of Lightnings airworthy. This P-38G of the 339th FS had suffered battle damage over the Treasury Islands on October 7, 1943, causing its pilot to belly-land on Vella Lavella island. Groundcrews have wasted little time in stripping the crippled aircraft of its vital guns and parts. (National Archives)

P-38H

With the production of the P-38H, engine power was increased to 1,425hp with the introduction of the Allison V-1710-89/91. The H-model was the first Lightning to be fitted with fully automatic engine controls, along with new turbo superchargers and automatic oil radiator flaps. These improvements gave the Lightning more power at high altitude and a maximum speed of 402mph at 25,000ft. The M1 20mm cannon was replaced by the M2 version and the underwing bomb capacity for both racks was raised to 1600lbs. 601 P-38H models were produced, with 90 being converted to the F-5B photo reconnaissance model.

P-38J

Introduction of the P-38J was a big step forward for the aircraft. Up to this point the basic contours of the Lightning, and its engine nacelles, had remained virtually unchanged. With the new J-model, however, "beard" or "chin" intakes had been installed directly below the propeller spinners. Earlier versions of the P-38 had been afflicted by compressed air cooling problems created by the turbo supercharging. If the air being fed to the latter was not cool enough, it duly restricted engine power at higher altitudes and created explosive backfires.

With the J-model, the old method of passing the compressed air through hollow passageways (intercoolers) fitted within the leading edge of the wings was replaced by core-type radiators located below the engines and sandwiched between the oil radiator intakes. The core type radiators were very efficient, and with the elimination of the

The brutal physical terrain and the disease-ridden climate of the Southwest Pacific imposed extreme hardship on all who served there. To make matters worse for groundcrews, virtually all aircraft maintenance was done out in the open. Keeping sophisticated machines like the P-38 airborne was a difficult task, and its success was directly dependant on the men who serviced them. They were the unsung heroes, and in this photograph Lightning armorers are working on 0.50-in. machine guns (left) and a 20mm Hispano cannon (right) somewhere in New Guinea. (National Archives)

leading edge ducting more space was created for additional fuel tanks – capacity was duly increased to 410 gallons internally. Although the new chin radiators created more drag, they finally allowed the Lightning to use full engine power at altitude. The P-38J, equipped with the same engines as the H-model, was the fastest Lightning of them all, with a top speed of 420mph at 26,500ft.

P-38J LIGHTNING NOSE GUNS

The Lightning's armament of four Browning M2 0.50-in. machine guns (with a total of 2,000 rounds) and one Hispano M1 20mm cannon (150 rounds) did not change throughout the war. The rate of fire for the 0.50-in. machine gun was 750rpm, while the figure for the 20mm weapon was 650rpm. The concentrated firepower from these five guns proved devastating, and few, if any, Japanese aircraft could withstand even a short burst from a P-38.

P-38Ls of the 318th FG line up for take-off from Isley Field, on Saipan, in November 1944. The P-38L was introduced during the second half of that year, the fighter being fitted with dive flaps and power-boosted controls. These additions made it the best, and most advanced, P-38 to see frontline service. (National Archives)

Production began in August 1943, and 2,970 J-models were built. Just prior to their construction run coming to an end in June 1944, the last 210 P-38Js were modified still further by Lockheed through the fitment of electrically operated dive-brakes (to offset compressibility) and a hydraulically actuated aileron boost system. The latter vastly improved the Lightning's rate of roll to the point where it boasted one of the highest of any World War II fighter.

P-38L

The P-38L was the most numerous of the all the Lightnings built – 3,810 by Lockheed and 113 by Consolidated-Vultee. Powered by 1,475hp Allison V-1710-111/113 engines, the L-model was capable of developing 1,600hp for each engine both at take-off and at 28,700ft. Apart from the more powerful engines, the P-38L was basically the same as the late production J-model.

Ki-61 HIEN

Ki-61-Ia

The first combat-ready Hien was the Ki-61-I Type 3. It was powered by the license built Ha-40 engine, which was a lighter version of the DB 601A rated at 1,175hp for take-off. Armament consisted of two Type 1 Ho-103 12.7mm machine guns mounted in the fuselage and two Type 89 7.7mm machine guns in the wings. The 7.7mm guns were of questionable value given that all US fighters were armored against this type of round. Add the fact that the two 12.7mm guns were synchronized to shoot between the propeller blades, and the Ki-61 had a weight of fire that was basically the same as the Ki-43-Ic Hayabusa. Thirty-four Hiens were built in 1942, after which production increased rapidly. A total of 1,380 Ki-61-Ia/bs were eventually built.

On June 1, 1944 Ki-61-Ia construction number 263 was given new Technical Air Intelligence Center (TAIC) serial number 9, which was painted on the fin, along with its real identity stencilled on the rear fuselage. The fighter's spinner was also given a coat of bright red paint at this time. The aircraft had been captured intact at Cape Gloucester, on New Britain, in February 1944 and initially shipped to Australia for flight testing by the Royal Australian Air Force's No. 1 Aircraft Performance Unit. It was then sent to the US and assigned to the TAIC at Naval Air Station (NAS) Anacostia, in Washington, D.C. (National Archives)

Ki-61-Ib

This version was identical to the Ki-61-Ia in all respects other than its armament, as the two 7.7mm weapons had been replaced by a pair of Type Ho-103 12.7mm machine guns. In mid-August 1943, 388 Ki-61-Ia/bs were modified on the assembly line to carry one German-built Mauser MG 151 20mm cannon in each wing. Space was limited in the wing so the new weapon had to be mounted on its side, with a small underwing fairing covering the breech. Some local strengthening of the wing was also required because of the increased recoil effect associated with the cannon. These modifications entered the production line in September 1943, but with only 800 Mauser cannon available the supply of the weapon soon ran out.

Ki-61-I KAIc

Reports from the frontline in New Guinea had shown that field maintenance had to be improved. The Ki-61's structure was strengthened and simplified, and with the availability of the indigenous Ho-5 20mm cannon the new Ki-61-I KAIc was born. With two Ho-5 cannon mounted in the fuselage, along with the two 12.7mm weapons in the wings, this up gunned version of the aircraft would be the most heavily armed single-seat Japanese fighter to see action in the South Pacific. In addition to the new armament, the Ki-61-I KAIc was 7.5-in. longer, featured a detachable rear section, had a fixed tail wheel instead of a retractable one and was equipped with a new fire extinguisher system. Production of the fighter began in January 1944, and 1,274 examples were built in 12 months.

Ki-61-I KAId

The Ki-61-I KAId was armed with a pair of Ho-105 30mm cannon in the wings and two fuselage-mounted 12.7mm machine guns. Only a few were built, however.

Another captured "Tony" somewhere in the Philippines in April 1945. By this time the Ki-61's secrets were well known, and wrecks like this one were no longer worth salvaging. This example is most likely a Ki-61-I KAId, which was heavily armed with two Ho-5 20mm cannon and two Type 1 12.7mm machine guns. (National Archives)

Ki-61-II

Soon after production began on the Ha-40 engine, the Kawasaki engineering team began work on a more powerful version – the Ha-140, rated at 1,500hp for take-off. Completed in December 1943, the first Ki-61-II had a wing area that was ten percent greater than the Ki-61-I. Pilot visibility was also improved with a redesigned aft canopy. Flight trials of the new variant proved to be extremely disappointing, however, as the Ha-140 engine had more than its fair share of teething problems and crankshaft failures. The fighter's handling characteristics were also poor, and its wing, which was designed for optimum performance at high altitude, suffered several structural failures too. Consequently, only eight of the eleven Ki-61-IIs built were ever test flown. The ninth airframe was modified as the Ki-61-II KAI before completion in April 1944.

Kawasaki's attempt to improve on the excellent Daimler-Benz DB 601A engine was a regressive step that ended in failure. Indeed, the Ha-140 as fitted to this Ki-61-II proved to be one of the most unreliable and troublesome piston engines of World War II. (National Museum of the USAF)

Ki-61-II KAI

The Ki-61-II KAI set out to eradicate the early problems that afflicted the Ki-61-II. Fuselage length was increased from 29ft 4in. to 30ft 0.58in., the rudder area was enlarged and the larger wings were replaced by the standard-sized wings of the Ki-61-I. When the Ha-140 performed well, the new Ki-61-II KAI was capable of some impressive numbers – 394mph at 19,685ft and an improved rate of climb that saw it attain 16,405ft in just six minutes. Confident that the Ha-140's problems would be solved, the Ministry of Munitions, acting on behalf of the JAAF, ordered Kawasaki to commence mass production of the Ki-61-II KAI in September 1944. The manufacturer duly built two versions of the fighter – the Model 2a, armed with two fuselage-mounted Ho-5 20mm cannon and two wing-mounted 12.7mm machines guns, and the Model 2b, armed with four Ho-5 20mm cannon.

The Ki-61-II KAI never supplanted the Ki-61-I in operational service, however, as issues surrounding both the engine's chronic unreliability and availability were never solved. Of the 374 airframes built, 99 Ki-61-II KAIa/bs were produced with the Ha-150 engine in the spring of 1944, but 275 airframes were left without engines.

Ki-61-Ia HIEN COWLING/WING GUNS

Initially, the Ki-61 was lightly armed, with the Ia version featuring just two Type 89 7.7mm guns in the wings and two Type 1 Ho-103 12.7mm weapons mounted above the engine. Rate of fire for the latter was 750rpm, and the Ki-61-Ia carried 250 rounds for each gun. The Ki-61-Ib was later up gunned to carry four 12.7mm machine guns, while 388 Ki-61-Ias and Ibs were modified on the assembly line through the fitment of a Mauser MG 151 20mm cannon in each wing – each gun could fire 120 rounds. By war's end the Ki-61-II KAI was armed with four Ho-5 20mm cannon, this weapon boasting an impressive firing rate of 850 rpm.

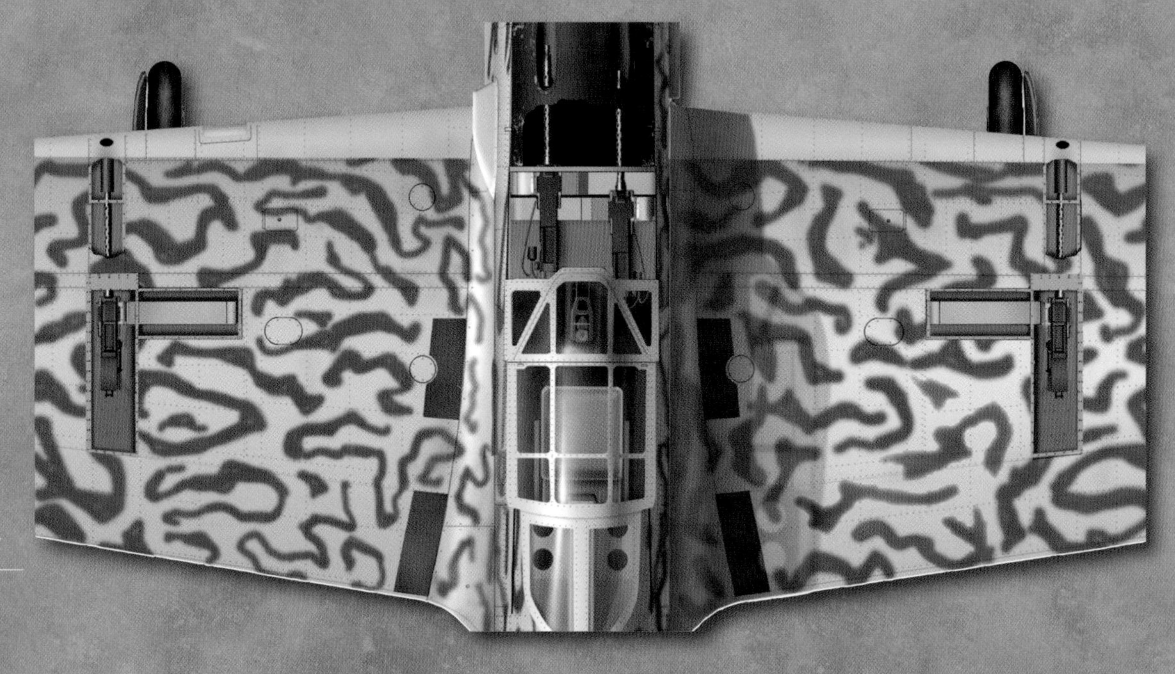

Born of desperation, the Ki-100 was armed with two 12.7mm machine guns and two 20mm cannon. The pilots who flew it considered it to be the best fighter employed by the JAAF. This particular aircraft belonged to the 2nd Chutai of the 59th Sentai, which began operations with the type in May 1945 at Ashiya. (Author's Collection)

Ki-100

The Ki-100 was a fighter born out of desperation. With Kawasaki unable to deliver its Ha-140 inline engines in sufficient numbers, the JAAF forced the manufacturer to adapt the existing engineless Ki-61-II KAI airframes to take the new and reliable Mistubishi Ha-112-II water-methanol injected radial engine of 1,500hp. The new prototype was completed in just 90 days, making its maiden flight on February 1, 1945. Initial flight testing went very well, and the JAAF quickly adopted it for service as the Type 5 Fighter, Model 1, Ki-100-I. The aircraft proved to be a great success, being one of the few examples of late-war Japanese technical and industrial prowess to enter widespread service. By the end of May 1945, the previously mentioned 275 engineless airframes had been redesignated as Ki-100s. While the fighter's top speed was slightly lower than the Ki-61, it weighed less, giving it a better rate of climb and much better maneuverability at higher altitudes. Its ease of handling also meant that it was a perfect mount for newly trained pilots, but by this late stage in the war it made little difference. Armament consisted of two 12.7mm machine guns and two 20mm cannon.

A VIEW FROM THE COCKPIT

Captured examples of the Ki-61-Ia were test flown by both the USAAF and US Navy during the war. In January 1944, the latter service tested a captured Hien against its top fighters. In a document titled "Final Report on Comparative Combat Evaluation Trials of Japanese Tony I Type 3 Fighter", the aircraft's cockpit environment was described as follows:

> Cockpit – The cockpit in the "Tony" is very small and cramped. However, the arrangement of instruments and control handles is good. The elevator tab is adjustable

in flight. The aileron and rudder tabs are adjustable only on the ground, and necessitate the continual use of rudder pressure in flight. The control handles for wheels, wing flaps, coolant and oil flaps, gun charging and hydraulic pressure are all located on the left hand side of the cockpit in a neat and convenient manner.

Vision – Vision in the "Tony" is not good. The long nose and relatively low canopy make forward vision extremely poor. Side and rear vision are fair. This aeroplane is not equipped with a bubble canopy. The visibility of US Navy fighter type aeroplanes is superior to that of the "Tony".

Armor – Two pieces, one behind the pilot used also as back of the seat, 0.5-in. thick, and one piece behind the pilot's head, again 0.5-in. thick."

P-38 Lightning and Ki-61 Hien Comparison Specifications

	P-38G	**Ki-61-Ib**
Powerplant	2 x 1,325hp Allison V-1710-51/55	1,175hp Kawasaki Ha-40
Dimensions		
Span	52ft 0in	39ft 4.5in
Length	37ft 10in	28ft 8.5in
Height	9ft 10in	12ft 1.75in
Wing area	327.5 sq. ft	215.278 sq. ft
Weights		
Empty	12,200lb	4,872lb
Loaded	19,800lb	6,504lb
Wing Loading	53.4lb/sq. ft	30.2lb/sq. ft
Performance		
Max speed	400mph at 25,000ft	368mph at 15,945ft
Range	850 miles	373 miles
Climb	to 20,000ft in 8.5min	to 16,405 ft in 5min 31sec
Service ceiling	39,000ft	37,730ft
Armament	4 x 0.50-in. Browning M2s 1 x 20mm Hispano M1	4 x 12.7mm Ho-103s

STRATEGIC SITUATION

Air combat in the Southwest Pacific was unique in many ways. In no other theater of war during World War II was air power more central to operations than here. As combat developed, it became clear that the objective of every major military move was to seize or neutralize an air base. Without control of the air, supplying such bases became next to impossible as everything had to be brought in either by ship or aircraft. For the Japanese, keeping their lines of communication open was vital for victory and, in the end, for their very survival.

Japanese aircrew assigned to the New Guinea theater described it as a "green desert" – a place from where one never returns alive. And sadly for the vast majority of them it was true. The air war in the Southwest Pacific was not only a battle of men and machines, it was also a struggle against a brutal climate, isolation and disease. For the Americans it was much the same, but fortunately for them they had a better industrial base from which to draw. In the end this allowed them to deal with the punishing environment more effectively.

By November 1942 the strategic situation for the Japanese was beginning to change. Their string of early victories in the first six months of the war had come to an end. The Battle of Midway on June 2, which had seen the IJN lose four aircraft carriers, was a disaster. By September 20 the Japanese army had withdrawn from the outskirts of the New Guinean capital Port Moresby, and on November 13-14 its attempt to land new army units on Guadalcanal failed when the invasion convoy was destroyed by the "Cactus Air Force". The situation in-theater, while still critical for the Allies, was showing signs of improvement.

ABOVE
P-38Fs of the 39th FS/35th FG are seen lined up at Port Moresby in March 1943. The unit had swapped its Airacobras for Lightnings in November 1942, and by the beginning of 1943 its official score stood at 20 aerial victories. By the second week of January the squadron had generated five P-38 aces. (National Archives)

RIGHT
80th FS/8th FG Lightnings await their next mission from Kila Field, Port Moresby, in September 1943. The aircraft to the right is P-38G-1 43-2212 *RUFF STUFF*, assigned to Capt Norb Ruff, who finished his tour with four victories to his name. The fighter to the left is P-38H-1 42-66506 *PORKY II*, assigned to unit CO Maj Edward "Porky" Cragg. Six of the latter pilot's fifteen victories were scored in this machine, including two of his three "Tonys". Cragg was shot down and killed in 42-66506 on December 26, 1943 fighting Ki-44 "Tojos" over Cape Gloucester. (National Archives)

First generation American fighters like the tricycle-undercarriage P-39 Airacobra, rugged P-40 Warhawk and F4F Wildcat had held the line in the Southwest Pacific and proven their worth against the much vaunted A6M Zero-sen and Ki-43 "Oscar". It would be the next generation of fighters that would take the fight to the IJNAF and JAAF and secure victory.

As the US Army was preparing to go onto the offensive and drive the Japanese from Guadalcanal, the first Lightnings arrived in-theater. On November 18, 1942 eight P-38Fs of the 339th FS/347th FG flew their first mission in the Southwest Pacific when they escorted a mixed formation of B-17 and B-26 bombers. The P-38Fs were engaged by IJNAF Zero-sens during the operation and claimed three of the Japanese fighters shot down – these were the first victories credited to the Lightning in the Southwest Pacific.

The introduction of the P-38 in this theater represented a major improvement in the capability of Allied air power. The fighter's high speed, high altitude performance,

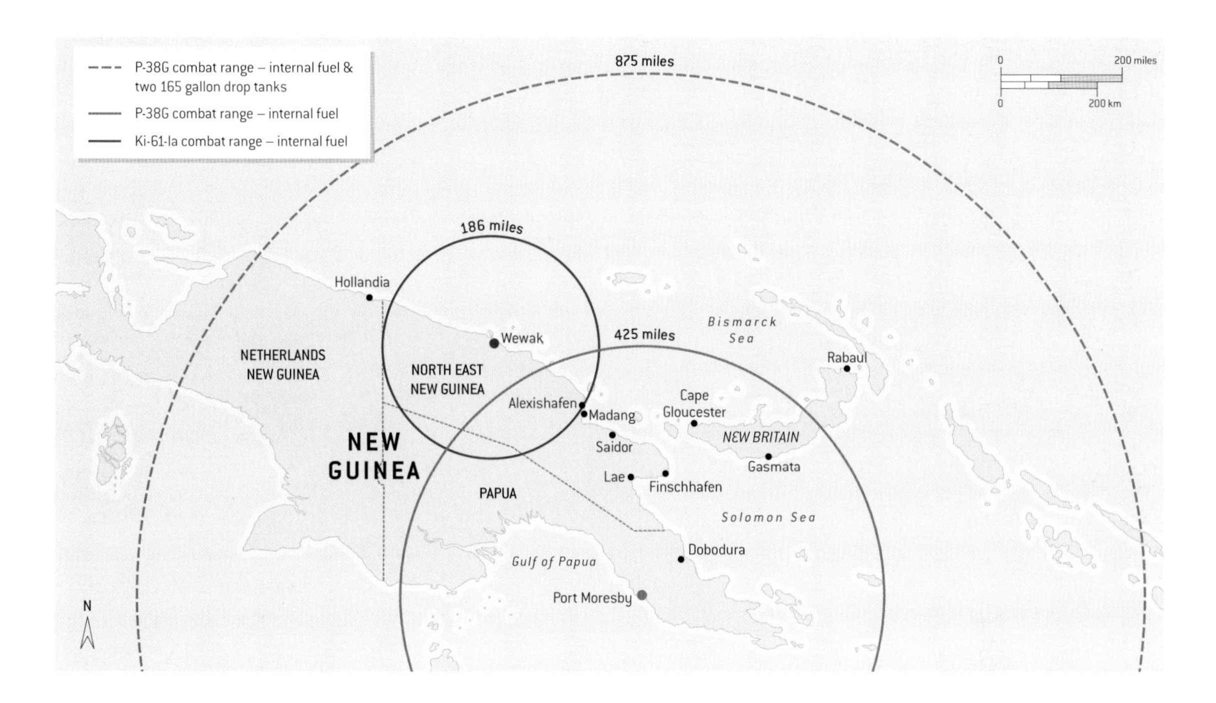

devastating armament and great range were far superior to anything the Japanese could field. But there were never enough Lightnings available. Due to the "Europe first" war policy adopted by the US government that saw forces committed to the fight in North Africa and the build-up of the Eighth Air Force in England, the majority of P-38 production was earmarked for these theaters. The Pacific would have to wait for the time being.

All frontline variants of the Lightning possessed outstanding endurance, which was a major factor in the fighter's success in the Southwest Pacific theater. The Ki-61, by contrast, had sufficient internal fuel for interception missions only. Combat range was measured as the distance to and from the target area. For the P-38G, that was 850 miles at 219mph at 10,000ft on internal fuel, or 1750 miles at 211mph at 10,000 ft with two 165US gal drop tanks. The Ki-61's range on internal fuel was limited to 372 miles.

Following the Lightning's introduction to combat in the Southwest Pacific with the 339th FS, the 9th, 39th and the 80th FSs all received sufficient quantities of P-38F/G to allow them to be declared operational with the Fifth Air Force by March 1943. Five months later the newly formed 475th FG was issued with 75 brand new P-38Hs as it became the first all-Lightning group in-theater. It would be these units that would take the fight to the Japanese across New Guinea and Rabaul in 1943-44.

By the late summer of 1943 the Japanese High Command realized that their position in the Southwest Pacific was tenuous at best. Their defensive campaign in the Solomons and New Guinea was turning into a shambles, and it would ultimately be described by postwar historians as Japan's "Stalingrad". In an attempt to reinforce their position, the JAAF began deploying aircraft to the region in late 1942, and even more were added (up to 100) in the summer of 1943. In June of that year the Japanese 4th Air Army redeployed from Rabaul to the newly constructed air base at Wewak, on the north coast of New Guinea. The majority of the Japanese fighter units in-theater were equipped with the obsolete Ki-43-II Hayabusa, codenamed "Oscar" by the Allies.

Desperate to bolster its forces in the region, the JAAF boldly decided to deploy the brand new Kawasaki Ki-61 Hien fighter to New Guinea. At the time there were fewer than 200 in service, and in many respects the Ki-61 was far from ready for combat

ABOVE
A factory-fresh Ki-61-Ia en route to Rabaul from Truk Atoll in the spring of 1943. Ferrying the Hien to the battle zone proved problematic, as JAAF pilots were not trained for over-water navigation. A number of Ki-61s were duly lost because of navigational errors during these early ferry flights. (National Archives)

operations. The need was so great, however, that the Japanese had no choice. At the time the Ki-61 "Tony" was the best, and only, fighter capable of meeting the P-38 on somewhat equal terms. It had good speed, could dive with the heavier P-40, was well armed for a Japanese fighter and was equipped with armor plate and self-sealing tanks. Its introduction to the new theater of combat was not an auspicious one, however.

RIGHT
Capt James A. Watkins of the 9th FS/49th FG stands with his right foot resting on the front wheel of his P-38G-10 42-12882 *Charlcie Jeanne*. To his left are the groundcrew that serviced his Lightning. Watkins had a habit of scoring multiple victories in single sorties, shooting down four "Tonys" on July 26, 1943, three "Oscars" two days later and three more on August 2. (via John Stanaway)

Having embarked in the aircraft carrier *Kasuga Maru* at Yokosuka in late March 1943, the 68th Sentai arrived at Truk Atoll, in the Western Pacific, on April 10. With its fighters offloaded, the unit despatched 13 Ki-61s to Rabaul a few days later, but only one reached its destination. Eight force-landed en route, two turned back and two simply disappeared.

By July 1943, both the 68th and 78th Sentais were operational with the Ki-61-Ia – one Sentai had approximately 42-49 aircraft assigned to it. Based at Wewak, these two units would subsequently bear the brunt of the fight with the Fifth Air Force's P-38 units. Suitable forward operating bases for Ki-61 operations were also set up at Madang, Alexishafen, Lae, Salamaua, Finschhafen and Saidor.

The 68th lost three more fighters and their pilots due to a navigational error while escorting bombers sent to attack Rendova on July 2. The 78th suffered its first losses shortly after this when two of its Ki-61s were written off in an accident during a bomber escort mission to Nassau Gulf. The fighter's first success came on July 18, shortly after both sentais had moved to Boram (Wewak East). The 78th Sentai engaged six P-38Gs from the 39th FS, and 2nd Chutai leader Lt Takashi Tomishima was credited with shooting one down. The Americans in turn claimed two Ki-61s destroyed, four probables and two damaged – the Japanese suffered no losses, however.

1Lt Stanley Andrews of the 39th FS "made ace" on July 21, 1943 when he downed one of the first two Ki-61s lost in combat in the Southwest Pacific. Both aircraft were from the 78th Sentai, which had 1Lts Kunji Fujita and Shoichi Ideta killed. The other "Tony" went to fellow ace 1Lt "Snuffy" Smith, who was actually credited with two destroyed. This date was also significant for the fact that the 39th FS became the first USAAF fighter unit in the Pacific to achieve 100 aerial victories. (Stanley Andrews)

On July 20 the 68th Sentai claimed its first victory when a B-24 was shot down over Bena Bena. Future ranking JAAF New Guinea ace Capt Shogo Takeuchi was leading the Sentai on this occasion. The next day, 18 fighters from the 78th Sentai were in combat with the 39th FS once again. Although five P-38s were claimed to have been shot down (three credited to Lt Tomishima, who also suffered a serious wound to his left arm that saw him hospitalized), the Sentai also experienced its first combat losses when two Ki-61s were downed by 39th FS aces 1Lts Stanley Andrews and Richard "Snuffy" Smith over Madang – the USAAF unit actually claimed three "Tonys" destroyed.

The Ki-61 Sentais endured terrible losses during the Allied bombing offensive on Wewak and But from August 16 onwards, losing aircraft both on the ground and in the air. The 68th suffered particularly badly on the 17th, when five of its Ki-61s were claimed to have been destroyed by the 475th FG. Four more were credited to the group on the 21st, after which the 68th Sentai was down to just two serviceable Ki-61s, while the 78th had none at all. Both units were withdrawn to Manila to re-equip – a pattern repeated several times up to year-end.

As the losses suffered by the two Ki-61 units in New Guinea in the latter half of 1943 show, the air war in the Southwest Pacific was very much one of attrition. While some of the world's most advanced fighters and bombers saw action in this theater, the basic maths remained the same – the side that destroyed the most aircraft prevailed.

As previously mentioned in this volume, the war in the Southwest Pacific often centered on the control of the few decent airfields in New Guinea and surrounding

Aces 1Lt Cy Homer (in P-38G-1 42-12705, coded "V") and Maj "Porky" Cragg (in P-38H-1 42-66835) escort B-25D-15 41-30594 of the 501st Bombardment Squadron/ 345th Bombardment Group as it heads for the Japanese stronghold of Rabaul on November 2, 1943. P-38s escorting B-25s proved a deadly combination. While the Lightnings kept Japanese fighters at bay, ground-strafing B-25 Mitchells (and A-20 Havocs) would be free to attack Japanese airfields at low level with devastating results. Cragg claimed a "Val" and a "Zeke" probably destroyed during this mission. (National Archives)

islands. A good airfield was worth its weight in gold, and here the Americans and Australians excelled. Their engineering prowess far outstripped that of the Japanese, allowing them to build airfields faster and better than their Japanese counterparts. By early 1943 Fifth Air Force had excellent sites from which to operate. In the Markham Valley in New Guinea, for example, engineers built a strip called Tsili Tsili. Its creation put short-range fighters within range of Lae and bombers within range of Wewak. In June of that same year Australian and American troops drove the Japanese from their once firm positions at Lae and Salamaua thanks to the air support provided by squadrons flying from Tsili Tsili. These same air assets then turned their attention on the JAAF at Wewak in August, as detailed earlier in this chapter.

In early November 1943 both sides began to reinforce their frontline strengths once again. Not only were numbers increased, but for the USAAF it also saw a significant

Rabaul takes a pounding on October 12, 1943. This photograph of Vunakanau airfield was taken by one of the many USAAF light bombers that attacked the Japanese stronghold. The original caption for this shot claimed the destruction of 200+ enemy aircraft on this mission alone. At least one of the "Tonys" seen here in their revetments is unserviceable, as the fighter has had its top engine cowling removed. (National Archives)

increase in quality. More P-38s began to arrive in-theater, and other squadrons replaced their seriously worn out P-39s and P-40E/Fs with new P-40Ns and P-47Ds. While paper strength listed the Fifth Air Force as fielding 600+ fighters in August 1943, approximately 200 were older machines that were not combat-capable.

On the Japanese side, while the JAAF was able to inject more aircraft into theater (the 68th Sentai returned to Wewak from Manila with 26 new Ki-61s in late November, for example), their poor serviceability rates created a situation where they had more aeroplanes than pilots.

By the late summer of 1943 the Japanese had realized their strategic position in the Southwest Pacific was on the verge of collapse. However, instead of a quick withdrawal into the Central Pacific and the East Indies, the Japanese continued to reinforce failure. As the Fifth Air Force progressively gained ground, smashing JAAF and IJNAF air assets both on their airfields and in the air, it became next to impossible for the Japanese to re-supply their distant bases. Yet they continued to try. Cargo ships in large numbers still made the trip to Rabaul throughout 1943, and some ran the gauntlet to Wewak until March 1944. It was a strategy that was destined to end in defeat, and one doomed to failure thanks in part to the remarkable qualities of the P-38 Lightning.

The Lockheed fighter's long reach, heavy firepower, excellent rate of climb and speed made it a treacherous foe for the Japanese. These attributes, combined with the sound tactics employed by the pilots who flew the P-38, meant that the Lightning groups held a distinct advantage over their JAAF counterparts equipped with the Ki-61. Lt Masao Oishihashi, an intelligence officer of the Ki-43-equipped 77th Sentai that fought alongside the "Tony" units in New Guinea, summarized his thoughts in respect to the Lightning in Interrogation Report No 600:

> We had a great respect for the performance of this aeroplane, and were amazed at its formation attacks, quick climbing ability and fine results achieved. Our fighters could not cope with the formation attacks, particularly when P-38s operated line astern.

At the beginning of September 1943, following the first Wewak bombing offensive, the Lightning-equipped 475th FG and 9th and 80th FSs were all based at Dobodura, while the 39th FS remained at Port Moresby. The construction of Dobodura airfield brought the war to the northeastern coast of New Guinea, setting in motion the strategic advances that would follow in late 1943. The JAAF (and IJNAF) had their main bases at Wewak, Hollandia and Rabaul, with forward airfields located at Madang, Alexishafen, Finschhafen, Lae, Cape Gloucester, Gasmata and Saidor – all well within range of marauding P-38s and Allied medium and heavy bombers.

THE COMBATANTS

AMERICAN PILOT TRAINING

During the first 18 months of the war the USAAF was under great strain. The demand for pilots in 1942-43 forced its training system to place an emphasis on "quantity rather than quality", and it was not until the early part of 1943 that Allied training surpassed Japanese training in terms of its length and overall quality. In the *US Strategic Bombing Survey*, commissioned by the Secretary of War on November 3, 1944 following a directive by President Franklin D. Roosevelt and published on July 1, 1946, the authors were quick to give credit, but they were also critical of errors they identified. In a report titled "The Air Campaigns of the Pacific War" their observations are enlightening:

> However, laboring under great pressure and in the fog of war, our military establishment did make serious errors in its training programs. It must be borne in mind that the training problem was gigantic. The Air Forces were expanding 100-fold and the ground and naval forces were also expanding greatly. Even though a tremendous task was accomplished in the training program, for the sake of future national security those mistakes which were made should not be overlooked. The two most serious errors are discussed below.
>
> The Numbers Racket – In general, the emphasis of our training program was on quantity rather than quality. In meeting deployment schedules and in prematurely committing forces to combat theaters, we became obsessed with the numbers of people and units produced, rather than with the state of their training. Particularly during the first two years of war, aircrews, specialists and units would have achieved a barely operable proficiency level when they were committed to active theaters. This was a false economy.

It actually delayed rather than accelerated the effective impact of our Air Forces on the enemy. Only a moderate increase in the training given to aircrews and technicians would have produced a much higher combat capability, and thereby would have reduced the logistic requirements and the overall structure required. We had not fully comprehended that a war of technology depends more on the efficiency and the skill of a relatively small number of people employing powerful weapons than on sheer weight of numbers of armed masses.

While the Americans had their problems, the report revealed that the situation for the Japanese was far worse:

The JAAF made a much more serious mistake in this matter than did our own military establishment. Lacking a general depth in their technological echelon, at all levels, the JAAF could ill afford to lose those technicians and specialists which had been trained in prewar years. It required much more time for Japan to train a replacement than for the United States. Having planned a war of short duration and limited objective, Japan had not provided the training organization to replace attrition losses with an acceptable product. Hence, the early losses suffered by the JAAF, both in pilots and technicians, confronted the enemy with an impossible replacement task. When Japan had lost her best pilots and technicians in the New Guinea-Solomons area, she had thereby lost the air war. While thousands of aircraft could be built, only hundreds could be maintained and only scores could be manned by pilots qualified to fight or bomb effectively.

Utilization of Civilian Skills – The second greatest weakness in our training program was a failure, in many instances, to utilize properly and build from civilian skills. This was not, however, exclusively a training problem or failure. Many factors, including our draft laws, worked to transplant highly qualified individuals from one line of productive war endeavor to other fields in which their specialties were not employed. One bright spot illuminating this situation, however, was the fact that utilization of civilian acquired skills was much better in World War II than in World War I. Nevertheless, it is mandatory that in a future war a system be established which will provide much better results than were obtained in World War II."

While there were deficiencies on both sides, it was the Japanese who failed to cope and were never able to recover – by mid-1943 they had clearly begun to crumble. It should also be remembered that while the Allies stabilized the situation in the frontline and were able to turn back the Japanese expansion, they did it with deficiencies of all kinds, especially in well-trained aircrews and combat equipment.

Training a fighter pilot for war and actually flying in combat are two very different things. Indeed, no amount of training can fully prepare a young man for the rigors of war. By early 1942 the USAAF's pilot training program was carried out by Technical Training Command and Flying Training Command, with potential pilots requiring a minimum number of flying hours before they could get their wings.

Tuition was undertaken in four stages starting with Primary Flight Training, which saw students accrue 65 hours in primary trainers such as the 200hp PT-19 Cornell monoplane

A young Lightning pilot poses for the camera as he enters his P-38D prior to undertaking a training flight somewhere in the US. This romantic image of the determined fighter pilot was in sharp contrast to the reality of combat that awaited him in the Southwest Pacific. The living conditions on the hot, humid, disease-infested islands were extremely difficult. Physical exhaustion, sleep degradation, poor diet, dehydration and the mental stress of combat all took their toll. Malaria and dysentery were common, as were a host of other diseases. Indeed, things got so bad in March 1943 that the Fifth Air Force's chief surgeon reported that "in some areas of New Guinea – Milne Bay particularly – malaria has become widespread. In some units as many as 35 percent of their personnel have contracted it in one month". (Author's Collection)

or 220hp PT-13 Stearman biplane. The standard primary school flight training was divided into four phases, with the pre-solo phase including general operation of a light aircraft, proficiency in landing techniques and recovery from stalls and spins. The second phase involved pre-solo flying and working on patterns such as elementary 8s, lazy 8s, pylon 8s and chandelles. The third phase was dedicated to developing a high proficiency in landing approaches and landings. The fourth phase dealt with aerobatics. Each cadet had to make at least 175 landings before moving on. This was followed by 70 hours of Basic Flight Training in a 450hp BT-13/15 Valiant basic trainer.

The next stage was Advanced Flight Training, which took the form of a ten-week course involving 75 hours of flying, 60 hours of ground schools and 19 hours of military training. Flying was done using the most powerful aircraft in the training syllabus, the 600hp AT-6 Texan. After successfully completing Advanced Flight Training the trainee would be awarded his silver pilot's wings and given the rank of flight officer, or commissioned as a second lieutenant. Transition flying training soon followed, with pilots learning to handle early versions of frontline single-seat fighters like the P-38, P-39, P-40, P-47 and P-51.

In 1942 the Lightning was the most advanced single-seat twin-engined fighter in the world. New pilots assigned to units equipped with it in the frontline had to learn

P-38L LIGHTNING

1. L-3 optical reflector gunsight
2. Hatch release handle
3. Hatch release buttons
4. Hatch locking arms
5. Cockpit light
6. Gun compartment heat control
7. 5-in. rockets fuse box
8. Standby magnetic compass
9. Suction gauge
10. Clock
11. Compass indicator
12. Directional gyro
13. Gyro horizon
14. Dual manifold pressure gauge
15. Dual tachometer
16. Mixture controls
17. Coolant shutter controls
18. Throttle levers
19. Reserve fuel tank gauge
20. Altimeter
21. Airspeed indicator
22. Turn and bank indicator
23. Rate of climb indicator
24. Port engine oil temperature, oil pressure and fuel pressure gauge
25. Coolant temperature gauge
26. Carburetor air temperature gauge
27. Circuit breakers
28. Flap control lever
29. Radio OFF push button and frequency selector push buttons
30. Recognition light switches
31. Elevator tab control
32. Bomb/tank release selector switch
33. Oxygen pressure gauge
34. Rudder pedals
35. Propeller feathering switch warning light
36. Oxygen flow indicator
37. Oxygen regulator
38. Parking brake handle
39. Dive recovery flap control switch
40. Control yoke
41. Control column
42. Aileron boost shut off valve
43. Window crank handles
44. Landing gear control handle
45. Detrola receiver tuning knob
46. Cockpit ventilator control
47. Starboard and port tank selector valves
48. Outer wing tank low-level check button and auxiliary fuel pump switches
49. Seat adjustment lever
50. Seat
51. Machine gun button (left) and cannon button (right)
52. Cockpit heat control
53. Propeller controls
54. Propeller selector switches
55. Microphone switch

This ex-British P-322-B was used as a trainer at Muroc Field, California, in 1942-43. American test pilots described the Lightning as "simple and pleasant to fly. However, the number of instruments and controls will give a new pilot the feeling that he is flying a complicated aircraft. The cockpit drill should be stressed and the inexperienced pilot should spend twice the normal amount of time sitting in the cockpit and studying the controls and instruments. If possible, a new pilot should spend a minimum of 30 hours in a single-engined fighter to build up his confidence, followed by several familiarization flights as a co-pilot in a twin-engined aircraft to help his twin-engined technique prior to flying the P-38 for the first time". (National Archives)

to fly an aircraft powered by two turbo supercharged engines, and understand the plumbing and cooling systems associated with these complex powerplants. The Lightning also had tricycle landing gear, which was considerably different, and safer, to the undercarriages fitted to the "tail-dragging" types pilots had previously trained on. Incredibly, during the early part of the war many tyro fighter pilots received just ten hours flying time in their new mounts before being assigned to their squadrons.

While it was a major, and frightening, leap for a young pilot to move from the 600hp AT-6 to a beast like the P-47 Thunderbolt or P-51 Mustang, it would have been even more overwhelming for those transitioning to the P-38. Dual trainers were non-existent and crashes were far too common. By today's safety standards the training was harsh and unforgiving, and in some ways it had to be. But the price paid proved devastating as thousands were lost learning to fly some of the world's most dangerous

This training flight ended in disaster when P-38E 42-2291 crashed just short of the runway at Paine Field, Washington state, on October 5, 1942. (National Archives)

and potent fighters – the USAAF recorded 52,651 training accidents resulting in 14,903 fatalities and 13,873 aircraft written off in World War II. Having survived the five-week transition training period, pilots were then assigned to unit training groups or designated as replacements bound for squadrons already in the frontline.

For newly trained pilots, understanding and being able to utilize the capabilities of his new fighter was the most important factor. Sadly, many early war American pilots arrived in the frontline with inadequate training, and in the dark days of late 1942 it was not unusual for some to have as little as 200 flying hours in their logbooks when they reached the frontline. Things rapidly improved from this point on, however, and between December 1942 and August 1945 no fewer than 35,000 day-fighter pilots were trained by the USAAF.

JAPANESE PILOT TRAINING

Like their IJNAF counterparts, JAAF pilots at the beginning of the war were, in the main, seasoned veterans with many hundreds of flying hours to their credit. The combat experience they had gained in China prior to Pearl Harbor was invaluable, and the early victories achieved by pilots flying the Ki-27 "Nate" and Ki-43 "Oscar" in 1941-42 was a clear example of their capabilities. By 1943 replacement pilots sent to JAAF sentais in New Guinea had on average the same amount of flight time as their Allied opponents.

After the war the Fifth Air Force conducted a study of JAAF pilots which concluded that they were well trained until early 1943. At this point a steady decline began that ended in November with the destruction of Wewak. During the first year of the conflict in the Southwest Pacific, pilots in-theater had good totals of 300-500 flying hours, but for much of 1943 the largest group comprised pilots with 200-300 flying hours. In November of that year a new group of replacement pilots arrived at Wewak with less than 200 hours each. By July 1944 only a handful of JAAF fighter pilots in the frontline had 300+ hours to their names.

Dubbed the "Cape Gloucester Ki-61", this particular aircraft was reputedly the mount of leading Hien ace Capt Shogo Takeuchi, commander of the 2nd Chutai of the 68th Sentai. By December 15, 1943 the latter unit was down to just three pilots when US forces landed at Arawe Peninsula. Escorting a small force of light bombers sent to attack the invasion beaches, Takeuchi was set upon by P-47s that severely damaged his aircraft (not this particular one). He crashed his Ki-61 when it suffered engine failure on the approach to Hansa airfield and succumbed to the injuries he had received in the accident three hours later. (National Archives)

Ki-61-Ib HIEN

1. Type 100 Gunsight
2. Turn and bank indicator
3. Compass
4. Rate of climb indicator
5. Airspeed indicator
6. Clock
7. Altimeter
8. Ho-103 12.7mm machine guns
9. Coolant temperature gauge
10. Oil temperature gauge
11. Oil pressure gauge
12. Fuel pressure gauge
13. Coolant shutter indicator
14. Oxygen flow meter
15. Fuel gauge
16. Engine fuel primer pump
17. Fuel tank changeover cock
18. Fuel injection pump
19. Landing gear indicator lights
20. Type 99 No. 3 wireless receiver
21. Rudder pedals
22. Hand-operated fuel pump
23. Wing-mounted gun cocking handles
24. Emergency landing gear release handle
25. Oil pressure pump handle
26. Emergency oil pressure changeover lever
27. Flap lever
28. Fuselage gun cocking lever
29. Radiator flap control lever
30. Landing gear lock safety lever
31. Landing gear lever
32. AC lever
33. Trim tab control lever
34. Control column
35. Throttle
36. Propeller pitch control
37. Fuel tank changeover cock
38. Tachometer
39. Manifold pressure gauge
40. Engine magneto switch
41. Outside air temperature gauge
42. Cockpit light
43. Seat
44. Electric control panel
45. Oxygen control lever
46. Machine gun trigger
47. Seat adjustment lever
48. Oil pressure gauge

Like all air forces during the war, the JAAF's training programs suffered from a high number of crashes and fatalities. In Air Intelligence Report No 251 produced after the war, a Maj Iijima gave his thoughts on both flying safety and accidental versus operational losses during the war:

> Maj Iijima stated that prior to Saipan, accidental losses of aircraft outnumbered operational losses by two-to-one. After Saipan, combat losses trebled, while accidental losses remained static, changing the ratio to approximately two-to-three.
> All Japanese training and accident personnel interrogated were asked what they would do to prevent aircraft accidents if given time, facilities and a free hand. Maj Iijima (representing the best informed JAAF viewpoint) proposed the following:
> "Wider and more effective use of motion pictures, posters and illustrated textbooks.
> "Voluntary enlistment (rather than conscription) of air cadets, resulting in a higher type of flying personnel.
> "Special training of instructors and supervisory personnel.
> "Organized flight control, with adequate ground radio facilities, and better radio equipment in aircraft.
> "Closer liaison between manufacturers and training personnel."

It is revealing that in all these categories the Allies were far superior.

After the war the USAAF studied the Japanese air training system and produced a detailed report, a portion of which follows:

> Individual Training of JAAF Recruits
> General – Recruits to the JAAF destined to become pilots normally pass through the following courses:

Another shot of Capt Shogo Takeuchi's Ki-61-Ia, seen here before its foliage "camouflage" had been removed. Manufactured in April 1943, this aircraft was sent to Australia for repairs and flight testing soon after its capture. Known by its construction number, 263, the fighter can be seen in Allied markings elsewhere in this volume. The broad white band behind the cockpit identifies this aircraft as belonging to the 2nd Chutai of the 68th Sentai. (National Archives)

Preparatory Training – 2 to 12 months
Elementary Flying Training – 8 months
Advanced Flying Training – 4 months
Operational Flying Training – 2 to 6 months

Preparatory Training
The length of this introductory training varies with the age of the recruit. Recruits of military age, and men transferred from other branches of the Army, receive a short two months "recruit training" course of a general nature, designed to provide an introduction to air force routine and inculcate a spirit of devotion to that service. Boy recruits on the other hand take a 12 months' cultural course in academic subjects, including science, languages, arithmetic and history. Physical training forms an important part of the curriculum. Not all graduates of these courses are destined to be pilots.

Elementary Flying Training
Eight months are spent at the elementary flying training schools, during the first six months of which all pilots-to-be train "en bloc" regardless of the type of aircraft they may eventually specialize on. During this period, flying time totals 20 hours dual and 70 solo, a biplane trainer being used. Before the conclusion of the course, recruits are separated into fighter, bomber and reconnaissance classes, and they spend two months converting to the special type of aircraft they will use at the advanced flying training centers. Flying time on this conversion course is reported to be 30 hours.

Advanced Flying Training
Pilots spend four months at an advanced flying training school, where instruction is given in formation flying, combat tactics, air-firing and night flying. Flying time here is reported to total 120 hours in advanced trainers, obsolescent operational types and a few first-line aircraft.

Operational Training
Having successfully completed their advanced flying training, pilots are then posted to an operational unit for operational training. This is supposed to last for six months, during which time pilots receive further instruction in combat tactics and become acclimated to local fighting conditions. Although six months is the stated training time, pilots are often required to participate in operations long before that time has expired. Flying times during this stage of training are unknown, although it is believed that efforts are made to raise the trainee's total to 400 hours at least before operations.

The system described above was insufficient for the growing needs of the war, and in 1942 it was supplemented by a second system providing additional facilities for advanced flying training. The latter eventually generated three times the number of replacement personnel turned out by the older system. The original training program was maintained, however, as a home organization, with the new syllabus being primarily designed to exploit training facilities overseas, although it was directed from Japan.

A Ki-61-Ia of the 37th Advanced Flying Training Unit at Formosa in 1944. To make up for the heavy aircrew losses in 1942-43, training capability was rapidly expanded and a number of overseas Advanced Flying Training Units such as this one were formed. (National Museum of the USAF)

In the autumn of 1943, in an effort to increase the flow of pilots, the War Emergency Organization was expanded through the implementation of conscription amongst students in universities and higher schools – classes hitherto exempt from compulsory service. Some 4000 teaching establishments are said to have been shut down in consequence. This large new influx of recruits was too much for the two existing training organizations to handle, and consequently in the spring of 1944 elementary flying training establishments were considerably enlarged and the Advanced Flying Training Regiments were increased in number from 18 to approximately 50. At the same time they were renamed Flying Training Units. Other training units were also formed to conduct specialist advanced flying training.

All these Advanced Flying Training Units (with the exception of about five) were located overseas, being divided, in the second half of 1944, almost equally between Manchuria, Korea, Formosa, the Philippines, Malaya and Java, and China. Their activities were directed, in each area, by Flying Training Brigades, which were in turn subordinated for operations to the Air Army in whose area they were located, and which was responsible for the training in its area.

By mid-1943 many officers, both USAAF and JAAF, agreed that replacement Japanese pilots were feeling the effects of the now emasculated training program. This revealed itself in the stark and unforgiving world of aerial combat. Good training was essential, not just for fighting but for survival as well. Flying an aeroplane with the power of a locomotive proved too much for many young replacement pilots. Most if not all their energy was directed at just keeping the aircraft in the air. Young pilots were simply overloaded with stimuli and unable to respond in the correct fashion. American pilots frequently observed that their JAAF counterparts exhibited a "suicidal lack of action" when attacked. They also observed the definite lack of alertness, and many Japanese pilots seemed frightened or bewildered when their formations were split up.

Pilot training for both the JAAF and IJNAF was slow in providing well-trained pilots to replace combat losses. By 1945 the threat of invasion of the Home Islands was Japan's primary concern. By the end of the war nearly 10,700 aircraft had been assigned to the kamikaze role, and the 18,000 pilots available for combat had an average of just 100 hours flying time each. By March 1945 all training was terminated.

CYRIL F. HOMER

Cyril F. Homer had six basic rules for combat:

ALWAYS clear your tail before firing.

ALWAYS try to use the element of surprise.

ALWAYS close in, and then use short bursts.

ALWAYS take advantage of sun and cloud cover.

ALWAYS hit the enemy where they are the thickest.

ALWAYS try to join with another friendly aeroplane.

These rules served him well, and from August 1943 to November 1944, while flying with the 80th FS/8th FG, he amassed 15 confirmed kills.

Born on April 29, 1919 in West New Jersey, Cyril moved to the west coast as a youth. He duly attended the University of California before joining the Army Reserves. Transferring to the USAAC for flight training, he graduated as a pilot from Luke Field, Arizona, as part of Class 42-J on October 30, 1942. Homer then transitioned onto the P-38 Lightning at Muroc Field, California, prior to being sent to the 80th FS at Mareeba, in Queensland, Australia, in February 1943. The unit was transitioning from the P-39 to the P-38 at the time of his arrival.

Homer had suffered severe injuries in a crash while racing motorcycles before the war, and when he was first posted to the 80th he had a noticeable limp. This did not instill confidence in the battle-hardened veterans of the squadron, one of whom was his flight commander, Norbert Ruff. The latter remembered thinking that the USAAF was scraping the bottom of the barrel by making a fighter pilot of this severe looking man with a pronounced limp – just two years earlier an aviation cadet had had to be in perfect physical shape to earn a commission. All reservations vanished, however, when Ruff saw the most unbelievable maneuvers executed by Homer's P-38 Lightning, eventually coupled with some excellent shooting once the squadron was sent back into combat over New Guinea.

Based at Port Moresby, the 80th had battled the Japanese in P-39 Airacobras since April 1942, but now the squadron was fully equipped with the P-38, and it returned to the frontline on May 16 1943. Homer probably destroyed a Ki-43 five days later, and finally claimed his first confirmed kills on August 21 when he destroyed two A6M "Zekes" and a Ki-61 "Tony" over Wewak. Another

"Zeke" fell to his guns on September 4, and Homer duly became an "ace" nine days later when he destroyed an "Oscar".

Accompanying the 8th FG from Port Moresby to its new base at Finschhafen in December 1943, Homer continued to claim kills on a regular basis over Wewak in the New Year, accounting for two "Oscars" (on January 18 and 23) and a "Tony" (also on January 23). Another Ki-61 was destroyed on March 30, and Homer enjoyed his career high on April 3 when he downed two "Oscars" and two "Tonys" over Hollandia while flying a brand new P-38J-15. "Uncle Cy", as the ace became known within the 80th FS, chalked up his 14th kill (a Ki-43) on July 27, and rounded out his aerial victories with yet another "Oscar" destroyed over Leyte on November 10.

By then Homer was CO of the 80th FS, having assumed command of the squadron from 22-kill ace Capt Jay T. Robbins on October 4. Homer remained in this post until May 9, 1945, and he returned home later that same month.

Maj Cyril Homer left the service at the end of the war, and passed away on August 7, 1975, shortly after attending an 8th FG reunion.

SHOGO TAKEUCHI

Very few Ki-61 pilots survived the carnage over New Guinea, as they were either killed in action, died of disease, starved to death or simply vanished into the thick and unforgiving tropical jungle in the face of Allied advances from late 1943. Included in their number was Capt Shogo Takeuchi of the 68th Sentai, who was almost certainly the leading JAAF ace over New Guinea. Born in 1918 in Kyoto, he graduated as a second lieutenant with the Army Aviation Academy's 52nd class entry in September 1939.

Showing great promise as a fighter pilot, Takeuchi spent the early war years serving with the 64th Sentai's 3rd Chutai, which was equipped with the Ki-43. Seeing action over Malaya and Singapore, as well as the China/Burma/India theater, he honed his dogfighting skills under the tutelage of the sentai's CO, 18-victory ace Maj Tateo Kato, and his Chutai leader, Capt Katsumi Anma (32 victories). Takeuchi's early prowess as a pilot was confirmed on January 31, 1942 when he shot down three RAF Hurricane IIs over Singapore. Three months later Takeuchi was transferred to the newly formed 68th Sentai. Later that year the unit converted to the brand new Ki-61 Hien fighter and prepared for its transfer to New Guinea. Autumn and winter were spent in training, and in December Takeuchi took over the 2nd Chutai as captain.

In April 1943 the 68th Sentai arrived at Wewak, via Rabaul. Almost immediately pilots identified, and complained about, the Ki-61's fuel and radiator problems. Despite these technical maladies, a five-aircraft formation from the 2nd Chutai, led by Takeuchi, claimed a B-24 Liberator destroyed to give the 68th Sentai its first victory. Air combat over New Guinea was unrelenting during the second half of 1943, and the 68th suffered accordingly. Many of its senior pilots were killed in action or grounded due to tropical illness, whilst the unit lost aircraft in the air, on the ground and to unserviceability due to a growing lack of spare parts.

Despite these hardships, Takeuchi continued to lead missions and steadily add victories to his tally. Wounded in action in October, he discharged himself from hospital after 15 days and returned to the skies with his body still swathed in bandages. By now Takeuchi was considered to be the hero of Wewak by his men, who cheered him when he gingerly climbed back into his Ki-61, adorned with 58 red eagle victory markings.

By early December 1943 the 68th Sentai had only three pilots left, and Capt Takeuchi's days were numbered. On the 15th of that month US forces landed on Arawe Peninsula on the southern coast of New Britain. The Japanese reacted quickly, despatching a force of light bombers escorted by Ki-61s, one of which was flown by Takeuchi. The formation was jumped by a large force of P-47s, and after claiming a Thunderbolt destroyed, Takeuchi's aircraft was damaged when he succeeded in fending off a P-47 that was attempting to shoot down 68th Sentai CO Maj Kiyoshi Kimura. Having been wounded in the clash, Takeuchi managed to nurse his fighter across the strait and back to New Guinea. As he approached Hansa airfield his engine seized and the Ki-61 crashed into the trees. Pulled from the wreckage mortally wounded, Takeuchi died three hours later.

According to Maj Kimura, Takeuchi had flown some 90 combat missions over New Guinea in six months and shot down 16 enemy aircraft and probably destroyed ten more. These victories were added to the 30+ he had claimed with the 64th Sentai. Although Takeuchi was posthumously promoted to the rank of major, a proposed individual citation for distinguished service was not realised.

COMBAT

P-38 LIGHTNING TACTICS

In almost every category the P-38 Lightning was far superior to anything the Japanese had in the air in the Southwest Pacific. The only category in which existing JAAF fighters excelled was in a slow-speed turning contest – and American pilots were no longer playing that game. In essence Japanese pilots wanted to slow the battle down and use their superior maneuverability to gain a shooting position. For their USAAF foes, it was the complete opposite – keep the speed up and never turn with your opponent.

With the introduction of the Ki-61, JAAF pilots could no longer turn sharply to avoid being shot down. While the Hien was a vast improvement over the Ki-43,

Well-worn 9th FS P-38G/Hs are prepared for their next mission at Dobodura, in southeastern New Guinea, in August 1943. "White 88" was assigned to Capt Clay Tice, "White 95" was Capt Bill Haney's fighter (note its flight leader stripes on the twin booms), "White 85" was flown by Capt Larry Smith and "White 84" was Capt Jim Watkins' mount. (Steve Ferguson)

On April 5, 1943 Capt Clay Tice's P-38G (flown by future eight-kill ace 2Lt John O'Neill) suffered a broken nose strut that in turn caused the gear leg to collapse upon landing at Dobodura, New Guinea. Tice, who would end the war as CO of the 49th FG, became the first American to land an aeroplane on mainland Japan when he set down his P-38L-5 – also named *Elsie* – at Nittagahara airfield on August 16, 1945 after his wingman had run low on fuel. The latter pilot landed shortly after his CO. (National Archives)

making it the best Japanese fighter in-theater, it was still handicapped when compared to the high-flying P-38. Five-kill Lightning ace Charles King of the 39th FS/35th FG had this to say about the Ki-61:

> The P-38 pilots all liked the "Tony". It may have been a bit faster than the current Jap fighters we were fighting, but we had plenty of speed to spare, and the "Tony" was a lot less maneuverable than either the Zero-sen or the "Oscar", so it was an easy victory when encountered. It also appeared, to our delight, that the pilots who flew them were not of the highest skill.

Not only was the next generation of American fighters superior (F4U Corsair, P-47 Thunderbolt and F6F Hellcat), their pilots also enjoyed better command and control and employed superior tactics.

The introduction of the P-38 to the Southwest Pacific theater in late 1942 gave the USAAF a distinct advantage. For the first time it had an aircraft that could take the fight to the enemy and win almost every time. Fifth and Thirteenth Air Force P-38 pilots would duly sweep the Japanese from the skies over New Guinea, turning Rabaul into a virtual graveyard for both JAAF and IJNAF units. While their numbers were small (in November 1943 there were still only five squadrons equipped with P-38s in the Fifth Air Force), their success ratio was of the order of 20-to-1.

At the start of the war the "finger-four", or four-ship, element was already being used by many US fighter units. This was broken down further into the two-ship element, which was what made the four-ship formation so successful. When combat was initiated it would be the section leader who flew the fighting aircraft while his wingman protected his leader from attack by other enemy aircraft. This allowed the section leader to concentrate on attack without having to worry about an enemy aircraft sneaking up on him from behind, below or above. For inexperienced pilots it was the perfect way to initiate them into combat. Their job was kept simple, and while still hazardous, it allowed them to develop their skills and gain valuable experience. The cardinal rule was "the wingman should never lose the element leader".

The two-ship element was also considered to be five times as powerful as two single aeroplanes flying alone. Later, P-38 squadrons would also adapt the string formation for attack. According to V Fighter Command's unofficial war manual *"Twelve to One"*, published in August 1945:

> When one gets over the target, the flights fall into the fighting formation. That is, each flight forms itself into a loose string. These strings are mutually supporting, and when they are weaving and crisscrossing, present an extremely difficult nut to crack.

Equipped with effective tactics and the right aircraft, the Americans also had the electronic advantage. The radios carried by World War II fighters were heavy and easily damaged, and the humid tropical conditions proved to be a maintenance nightmare. Nevertheless, the radios were indispensable when using the four- and two-aeroplane element in combat. Indeed, the new tactical formations employed by US pilots in-theater would not have worked without the critical radio link. This allowed coordinated maneuvers both before an engagement and during the battle itself.

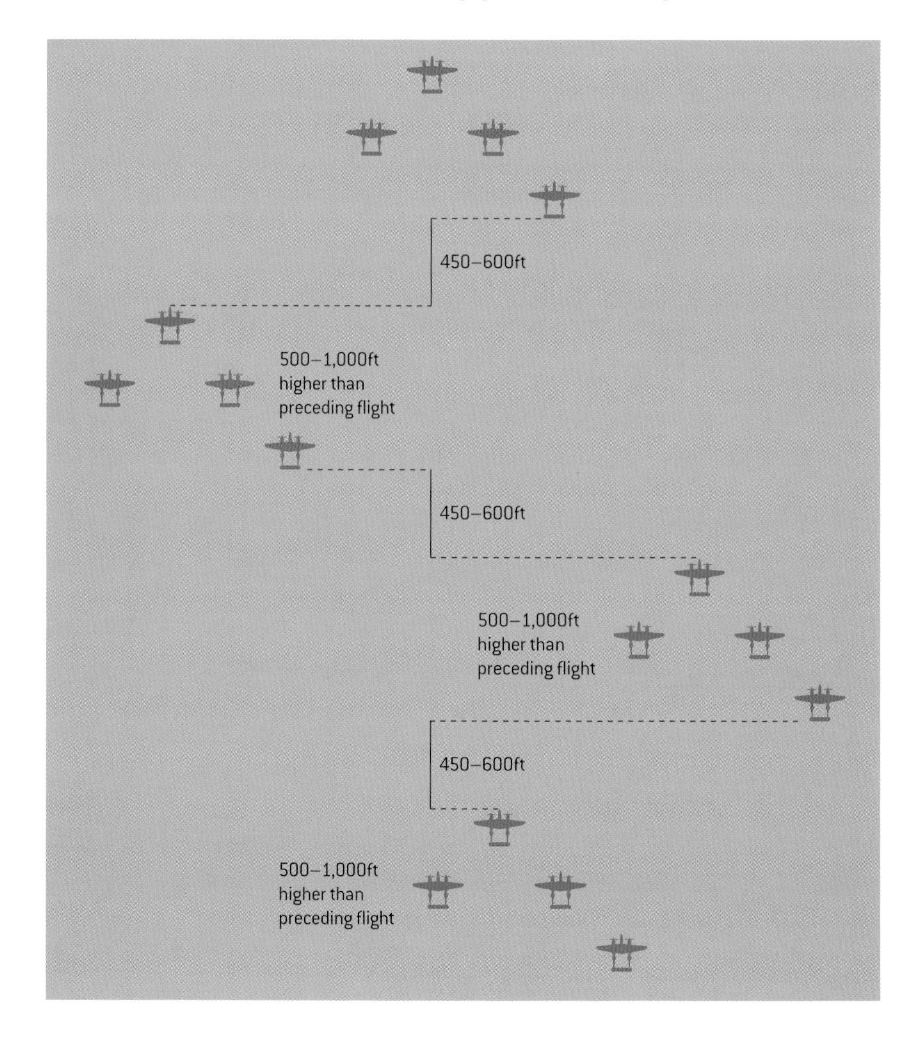

RIGHT AND OPPOSITE TOP
All Lightning units used the standard "finger-four" or four-ship formation from the very start, the USAAF having adapted it from the German four-aeroplane *schwarm* that resembled four fingertips outstretched. This formation was both extremely flexible and very effective. Aircraft were separated by 600-1,000ft, which was roughly equal to the Lightning's turning radius. The formation was led by a flight leader and his wingman, accompanied by a section leader and his wingman. During an attack, the formation usually broke up into two sections to continue the engagement.

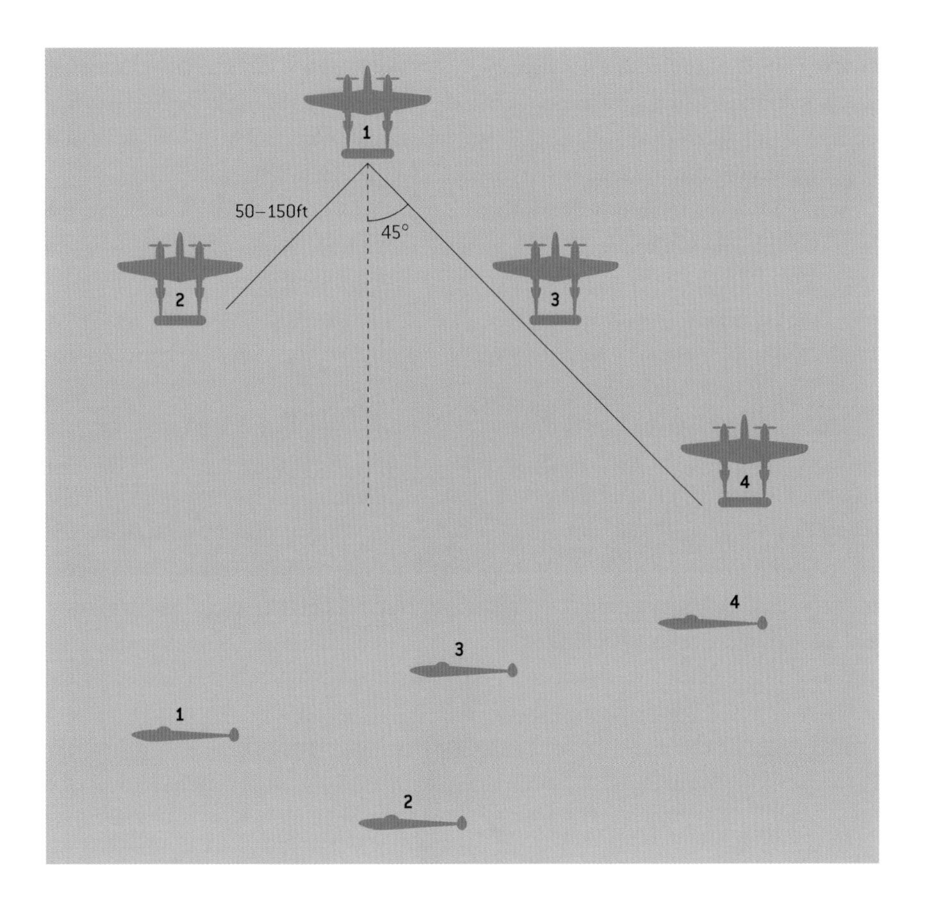

Instead of always looking for a visual clue from the flight leader, the quartet of pilots in the "finger-four" formation could devote their energy to scanning the sky. Radios also allowed warnings to be issued quickly, saving many lives, and when the battle was over pilots would use them to find fellow flyers and form up for the flight home in order to offer each other mutual protection.

For the Japanese, aeroplane-to-aeroplane radio communication simply did not exist. The radios in their fighters were so poor that they were simply taken out in order to

Four P-38Ls from the 431st FS/475th FG illustrate the highly effective "finger-four" formation (tightened up here for the camera) on a patrol from Dulag in mid-January 1945. (via John Stanaway)

save weight. But not all of their fighters flew without radios. Shotai or flight leaders would have a radio to communicate with their base, leaving the rest of the flight to rely on traditional visual clues. Flying high performance fighters and forced to use World War I communication techniques greatly hindered Japanese fighter tactics.

While having a distinct technical and tactical advantage, the P-38 pilots in the Southwest Pacific had to rely on their eyesight in the end. Seeing the enemy first was vital for success. The sky in the South Pacific was unusually clear. Unlike the skies over Europe, which were often covered with industrial haze, the skies in the Southwest Pacific allowed for visual contact to be made at great distances. Pilots with exceptional eyesight were some of the most successful.

Once contact was made and the enemy identified, the first thing to do was gain altitude. The trick was to create an altitude advantage and then try and trade it for speed in a diving attack. Here, the P-38 usually held the upper hand. Its high altitude performance and good rate of climb allowed USAAF pilots to dive through a Japanese formation, go into a shallow high-speed climb to gain superior altitude and repeat the process all over again. This technique almost always broke up enemy formations and allowed the enemy to be picked off.

The altitude advantage also allowed the Americans to choose when and how long they would fight. If a single pass was all they could accomplish, it was always better to fight another day than risk destruction by an unseen enemy aircraft or quickly changing tactical situation. Here again disciplined radio communications proved vital for success. Six-kill P-38 ace Maj Wallace R. Jordan of the 49th FG had these thoughts on tactics:

> Primarily, one principle which underlies the successful application of all the following fighter-to-fighter combat tactics with the Japanese is the neutralization of the excellent maneuverability of his aeroplane. In my experience, maneuverability is the only quality in which the enemy excels, and when allowed, he will use it to its fullest extent. Neutralization is effected simply by fighting in a manner that does not allow him to use his maneuverability.

This partially unpainted 39th FS P-38H has been placed on jacks so that it could be repaired by the personnel of the 27th Air Depot Group at Port Moresby. Photographed on October 7, 1943, this aircraft features a distinctive "sharksmouth" on its right engine nacelle. This marking was a carryover from the unit's time flying Airacobras. American maintenance capabilities for outstripped those of the JAAF fighter sentais in New Guinea, who had to fly their Ki-61s all the way back to the Philippines when they required an engine change! (National Archives)

Individual Defensive Tactics

First, do not attempt to dogfight. If you do, your chances are minimized by allowing the enemy to use maneuverability.

When enemy contact is imminent – i.e. over a target – maintain an indicated air speed of at least 250mph. From this speed, increased settings will quickly give you the necessary high speed when needed. Upon being attacked, several things can be done according to the type of attack. If seriously outnumbered, and attacked from above, establish a shallow dive at War Emergency setting until out of danger. If attacked from below, use a high-speed shallow climb. The enemy climbs more vertically and cannot stay with you in this type of climb.

At any time, your best individual defensive action is to rejoin another friendly aeroplane and use the team work of the two-ship element for mutual protection.

Maj Wallace Jordan, CO of the 9th FS, finished his tour of duty with six kills to his credit. Although he tangled with Ki-61s on a number of occasions, he never actually claimed one destroyed. (via William Hess)

Individual Offensive Tactics

When individually attacking an enemy fighter, use the speed necessary to prevent over-running, come from sun or cloud, and do not fire until minimum range is reached, unless the enemy fighter aircraft starts evasive action before that time. With premature firing, your ammunition is wasted by your tracers, prompting the enemy to take evasive action that you cannot possibly follow. The best pass, if you can get set for it, is to come in directly behind and slightly below.

The majority of Japanese pilots dislike the head-on pass and will not press it to minimum. If one does, your superior firepower will give you a distinct advantage.

Maj Jordan's insights into the P-38's armament reveal an excellent understanding of air-to-air gunnery:

Another aspect of this case is concerned with hot guns, and the resultant swirling of rounds there from. Following any amount of sustained shooting, your guns need at least ten minutes of cooling. If they are not given this cooling, the rounds will swirl, going in every direction and you will hit nothing. When the swirl is observed, pull off and allow someone else to take over the attack until your guns have returned to normal. Actually, your guns won't get the chance to overheat if you coordinate properly with the rest of the flight or element, because the target's evasive actions will change his attacker frequently."

80th FS ace Maj Cyril F. Homer was responsible for five "Tony" victories in the Southwest Pacific. His thoughts on how to shake a "Tony" off your tail also featured in *"Twelve to One"*:

Looking around, keeping your ship rolling and turning, is the best possible defense. As long as you see the enemy, his chances of nailing you are very slim. But in the case where

ENGAGING THE ENEMY

The P-38's armament was unique amongst American World War II fighters, as it was the only one to boast a mix of machine guns and a 20mm cannon mounted in the nose. The Lightning's clustered nose armament made it relatively easy for pilots to point the aircraft and fire with a fair degree of accuracy. In a two-second burst, a P-38 could unleash 50 0.50-in. shells and ten 20mm explosive rounds. For the lightly-built Japanese fighters and bombers that were the fighter's targets, it proved devastating.

When the P-38 fired its weapons the aircraft emitted a tight stream of rounds. Compared to other single-seat fighters, which had their guns mounted in the wings, the P-38 had a distinct advantage. Weapons mounted in the wings of a fighter had to be adjusted so that the bullets would strike a convergence point in front of the aircraft (usually at 1,000ft). Once fired from the guns, the bullet stream would converge inward and meet at the convergence point. Having past that point, the bullets would scissor outward. For P-38 pilots, convergence was not a problem. While all other fighters were producing cones of fire, the Lightning could strike its target with maximum effect. The P-38 could also strike at a much greater range.

Standard armament of a US fighter was six 0.50-in. machine guns (eight in the P-47 and only four in the P-51B/C). The destructive power of these guns depended on kinetic energy. The closer you were the more damage would be created (explosive cannon shells were less influenced by range). With converging fire there were pluses and minuses. For the expert marksman, a short burst near or at the convergence point produced the desired results. For the average pilot, a broader cone of fire raised his chances of hitting a target. An enemy aircraft caught in the cone of fire was in extreme danger. The air was full of bullets, and it did not take many rounds to cripple or fatally damage a Japanese aeroplane.

Having enjoyed success with both the P-38 and P-40K/N, 14-victory ace Capt Robert DeHaven of the 49th FG describes the pros and cons of converging fire:

"It was very hard to hit another aircraft in flight, particularly when you were using converging fire. By definition, it gave you one point of maximum impact at a particular boresight range – normally about 250 yards for the 0.50-in. Inside that boresight point and outside, you were effectively hitting with misses! In a P-38, however, you had parallel fire with the four "0.50s" and the 20mm going straight out in front of you. You didn't have to worry about a boresight point, as you always had maximum fire in the normal stream. A good shot could strike at a somewhat greater range in a P-38 than in any other fighter for this reason."

you have not done this and find your tail is dirty, then is the time to get violent on the controls. A violent combined push-over and roll to the vertical position will likely throw him off until you pick up diving speed. Twist, roll, reverse and jink until you have 400mph or more – in case it's a "Tony", that figure should be closer to 500mph – before pulling out level. Then you can easily outdistance him at this angle, or better yet, pull up into a shallow climb. Judge your lead carefully and reverse 180 degrees to him for a head-on pass, unless he is followed by some of his friends.

American pilots also used the head-on attack as part of their fighter repertoire. The concentrated nose armament of the P-38 made it especially devastating. Maj Cyril Homer had this to say:

In a head-on pass, bore in and don't budge until collision appears inevitable. You should have done him in by this time, but if not, push under violently.

When it came to long-range escort, the P-38 was in its element. Its high speed and high altitude performance almost always gave the fighter the advantage. One of the best tactics devised by the Fifth Air Force was to send a small force of P-38s "in high so as to attack any enemy formation. This causes them to break up into small units that can then be easily taken care of by the main body of escorting fighters. This group of aeroplanes should be about five minutes ahead of the main striking force".

The Japanese had no answer to the high-flying P-38s. Combined with their lack of efficient and reliable radar and completely inadequate air-to-air radios, their attempt to stop the Allied air offensive was a disaster.

Ki-61 HIEN TACTICS

Tactically, USAAF fighter groups were far superior to their JAAF counterparts. Their ability to adapt quickly was a testament to their fighting philosophy and training. While they had adopted the "finger-four" formation, the Japanese were extremely

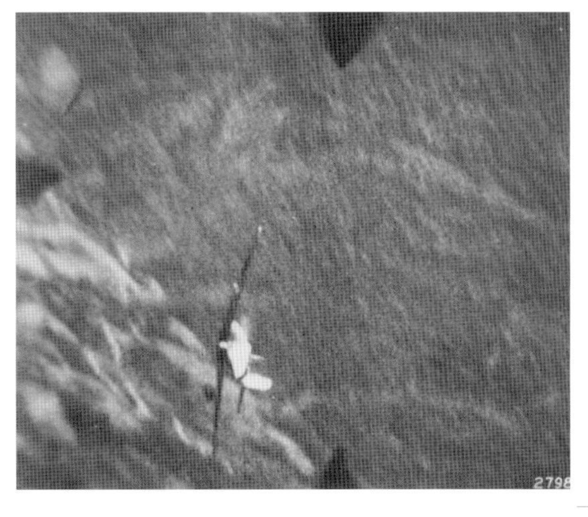

It would take gun camera film confirmation to correctly identify the new Kawasaki Ki-61 once it had made its combat debut in New Guinea in July 1943. Pilots encountering the aircraft for the first time swore that it was an "Me 109". The image to left shows a Ki-61 making what appears to be a head on attack, while the second still captures a Ki-61 diving away with a drop tank still attached to the underside of its right wing. (*National Archives*)

A damaged Ki-61 of the 78th Sentai is examined in western New Guinea in the spring of 1944. More "Tonys" were destroyed on the ground by marauding Allied aircraft than were shot down by fighters. This was a direct result of the Ki-61's poor serviceability record. Engine failures, chronic overheating problems and ineffective radiators made the "Tony" a maintenance nightmare. As a result these grounded aircraft proved easy targets for strafing B-25 and A-20 medium bombers. (National Archives)

slow to see its advantages, and therefore stuck with their "insect swarm" or gaggle formations. This may have been necessary due to the lack of good radios, but the idea of demanding and producing such equipment never seemed to occur to Japanese pilots. It appears that the doctrine of attack superseded anything else.

Japanese combat experience in China and against the Soviets in the 1930s greatly influenced, and hindered, JAAF operations in the Southwest Pacific. The lessons learned while fighting the feeble Chinese Air Force only encouraged Japan's great emphasis on individual dogfighting tactics. The introduction of the A6M Zero-sen and Ki-43 solidified the IJNAF and JAAF belief in the idea that a highly maneuverable fighter would always reign supreme. It was a philosophy that would inevitably lead to calamity and destruction.

The JAAF did, however, develop and improve upon the standard vee-formation. The Japanese three-aeroplane section was called a shotai, and it was a much more flexible formation than any other variety of the standard Vic. Instead of three aircraft flying in a rigid V, the leader would hold a steady course while two wingmen flew farther back. From their position the two wingmen would weave right and left and up

A close up of the Hien's camouflage pattern – in this case the "Cape Gloucester Ki-61". Aircraft assigned to the New Guinea front were painted by the Army Aviation Supply Depot in Gifu, Japan. No strict instructions were given as to how the dark green paint should be applied, hence some aircraft had a snake pattern while other camouflage schemes were more mottled or spotty in appearance. (National Archives)

2Lts Ken Taylor and George Welch claimed six victories between them when Pearl Harbor was attacked on December 7, 1941. Although Taylor failed to add to his score, "Wheaties" Welch claimed three more kills in a P-39D exactly one year later, followed by nine flying P-38G/Hs with the 80th FS/8th FG during the summer of 1943. Amongst his Lightning victories were a trio of Ki-61s downed near Wewak on August 20, 1943 (an extract from his combat report for this mission appears in the text on page 65). Joining North American Aviation as a test pilot in 1944, Welch's postwar career saw him perform the first flights of the P-82 Twin Mustang and F-86 Sabre. He was killed in a crash at Edwards AFB on October 12, 1954 while testing the new F-100 Super Sabre. (via John Stanaway)

and down. This gave the formation a great chance to spot a surprise attack and respond quickly. And when engaged in an attack the leader would be followed in trail by the two remaining fighters, each attacking in succession. When well coordinated, and several shotai participated, it was a devastating form of attack.

While this worked well in the attack mode, when the shotai was the victim of an attack Japanese pilots always fought individually. This system remained workable for several years, but in the end the Japanese failed to develop disciplined techniques for the effective use of their limited fighter resources.

JAAF formations, above the level of the shotai, were a constant mystery to the Americans. In after-action reports USAAF pilots often described Japanese formations as "swarms of bees" or "gaggles of birds", with individual aircraft flipping on their backs to check underneath the formation. This lack of discipline and good tactics gave the Americans a distinct advantage, as small groups of USAAF fighters could almost always scatter a larger Japanese formation, forcing the JAAF to fight as individuals, and thus playing right into the enemy's hands.

It is ironic that when one compares the national character of Japanese and American fighter pilots, it is the former, with their deeply ingrained group ethic, who emphasized the individual in air combat. For the Americans it was the complete opposite. Their small group tactics and belief in working as a team went against their belief and respect for "individualism".

The Japanese communication network was also at a disadvantage. Compared to American radar and the Coast Watcher system, the Japanese system was crude, although it was quite effective nevertheless. The Japanese did not need Coast Watchers due to the fact that they occupied dozens of islands in the Solomons and territory along the coast of New Guinea, all of which were ideally placed for observers. Japanese land radios were excellent, so an enemy raid could be quickly relayed back to base. Large Japanese bases also had radar, but their systems tended to be unreliable, in

FOLLOWING PAGE
The "shotai" was a more flexible version of the standard Vic formation, being more fluid and less rigid as the two wingmen flew farther back from the leader. While the leader held a steady course, the wingmen weaved left and right and up and down. This allowed the weaving fighters to check blind spots, giving the formation a much better defense against surprise attacks. The JAAF did not adopt the standard "finger-four" formation as used by virtually all other air arms until 1944.

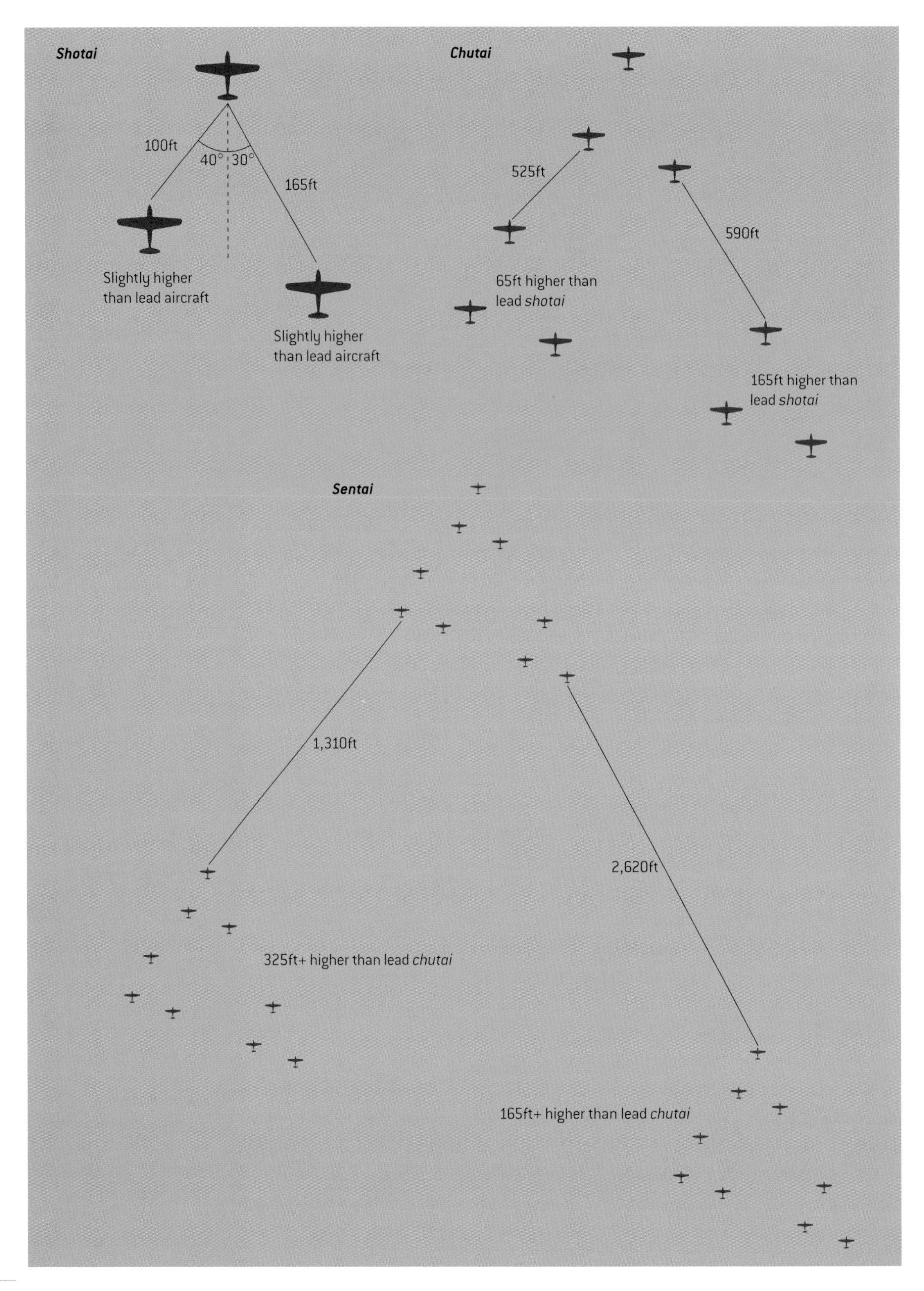
Shotai
100ft
40°
30°
165ft
Slightly higher than lead aircraft
Slightly higher than lead aircraft
Chutai
525ft
590ft
65ft higher than lead shotai
165ft higher than lead shotai
Sentai
1,310ft
2,620ft
325ft+ higher than lead chutai
165ft+ higher than lead chutai

short supply and their range of about 150 kilometers being shorter than comparable Allied units.

Detecting a raid was not the problem, however. Where the JAAF really struggled was in command and control of its fighter assets. Japanese airborne radios were so poor that vectoring was almost impossible. Instead, the JAAF had to rely on the World War I tactic of generating standing defensive patrols throughout daylight hours. While the Zero-sen and "Oscar" could stay in the air for a long time, the short-range Ki-61 could not. More often than not the patrolling fighters would be caught either returning to base or on the ground being refueled.

The introduction of the Ki-61 into the Southwest Pacific theater in mid-1943 did little to change the balance of power. In many ways the "Tony" was a good machine, but it sacrificed the one thing Japanese fighters excelled at. While its characteristics mirrored those valued by the Allies – good speed, the ability to roll quickly and dive, combined with increased armament and armor plate – it could not turn like the "Oscar" or Zero-sen. Its poor rearward visibility was also a major setback.

With the introduction of the Ki-61, Allied pilots could no longer use their superior diving capabilities. Faster than the P-39 and almost equal to the P-40 in a dive, American pilots soon found the "Tony" a hard opponent to shake when in a dive. Pearl Harbor veteran and 16-kill ace Capt George S. Welch of the 80th FS/8th FG discovered this at firsthand on August 20, 1943 over Wewak during an engagement in which he claimed three Ki-61s destroyed. His combat report stated:

> Close Cover for 24 B-24s on bombing mission to Wewak. At 1100 hrs I saw from 15 to 20 bandits at 22,000ft over Wewak. The bombers I was escorting turned around and I stayed with them. They made another pass, and 15 or 20 in another group intercepted us. They attacked individually, and one of them collided with a B-24 which exploded over Wewak. I made three 90-degree deflection shots and one 0-degree deflection shot at four enemy aeroplanes – all "Tony" type. They all turned to the left and climbed except one, which turned right and dived. I saw three crash – one in the town of Wewak, one behind and one east of Wewak point.
>
> One "Tony" dived on me from above and behind at about 22,000ft. I could not lose him with everything forward and 260mph indicated air speed. By climbing at 250mph I lost him, I believe. I returned home at 24,000ft at 1600rpm and 20 inches Hg (mercury) and landed with 60 gallons of gas.
>
> During the combat I saw a "Zeke" or "Oscar" spin in, crashing near the beach between Wewak point and the strip at Wewak. I claim three "Tony" aeroplanes.

While the Ki-61 was clearly superior to the obsolete Ki-43, the attitude and methods of the JAAF remained cruelly ineffective and hard to explain. In New Guinea, both the 68th and 78th Sentais were used primarily in the defensive role in an effort to protect Wewak from USAAF bombers. Their limited range excluded them from long-range escort missions, so most of their sorties were flown close to base. Yet the Japanese had no formal policy of air-sea-rescue for downed pilots. Experienced pilots and leaders lucky enough to bail out were left to their fate. The combat

FOLLOWING PAGE
On April 12, 1944 the 80th FS was assigned to escort B-24s that were targeting Japanese positions in Hollandia. The unit rendezvoused with Liberator bombers at 14,000ft, and a short while later its ranking ace, Capt Jay T. Robbins, spotted a gaggle of Ki-61s at "nine o'clock high". During the ensuing dogfight Robbins claimed "two definites and two probables" – all "Tonys". His last victory was the most dramatic, as he described in the following extract from his combat report. "I got two passes at him but couldn't get a very good shot, so I pulled up just north of Hollandia Strip at about 3,000ft and saw one ("Tony") turn right and down. He saw me and started diving and turning. After I worked him down very low, he turned a couple of times, then headed right for Hollandia strip. He didn't turn any more and went right down the strip. I drove right up on his tail and knocked him down right on the strip. He burst into flames. The B-24s were still bombing, and bomb bursts were all around me". This victory took Capt Robbins' score to 18 victories, and he would end the conflict with 22 kills to his name.

RIGHT
This photograph graphically illustrates just how complete American air power was over New Guinea in October 1943. With its bomb-bay doors open and engines at full throttle, a B-25 Mitchell roars over Borum airfield, near Wewak, with a lone Ki-61 of the 78th Sentai parked in the foreground. Behind it is a Ki-57 "Topsy" transport, and off to the side of the field is the centre section of a second "Tony". The fact that this B-25 is flying so low indicates that Japanese air defenses had by then become totally ineffective. (National Archives)

effectiveness of units would suffer accordingly. The total disregard that the Japanese High Command had for its soldiers and airmen in the field played a major role in their final defeat, for it is estimated that American PBY Catalina flying boats saved some 540 downed Allied pilots in the Southwest Pacific. It was not uncommon for Japanese airmen to watch as Allied aircrew were rescued within reach of their own shore-based artillery and vulnerable to fighter attack.

There was also no policy of rotation for pilots and groundcrews. Like their German counterparts, Ki-61 pilots flew until they were killed, wounded or evacuated due to disease. The latter was exacerbated by the starvation and neglect that afflicted Japanese forces in New Guinea. While their American counterparts also faced the same tropical diseases, they were better equipped to deal with the problem. The Allies sprayed and dusted their bases with the insecticide DDT, for example.

BELOW
This illustration was produced by the Fifth Air Force to illustrate the deployment of air assets over Rabaul during a raid on November 2, 1943. The Fifth Air Force claimed no fewer than 42 Japanese aircraft shot down by Lightnings of the 9th, 39th and 80th FS and the 475th FG on this date. (National Archives)

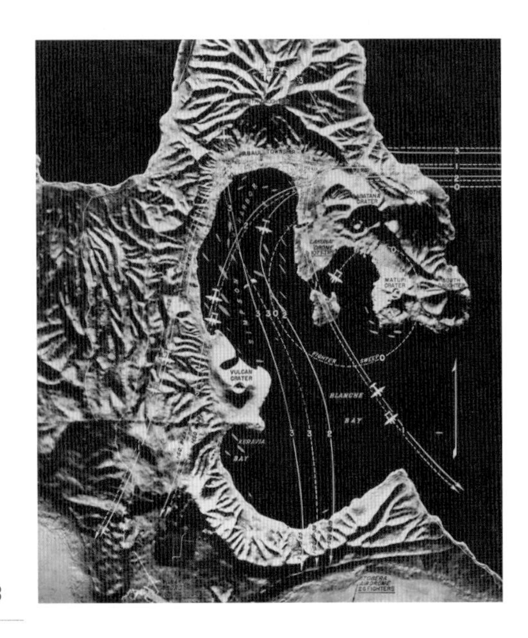

For JAAF pilots based in New Guinea, their combat effectiveness was directly influenced by the medical care available. In mid-1943 Allied pilots noted a sharp decline in the skills of their opponents. Some of that decline can be attributed to reduced training standards, but most certainly some of it was a direct result of debilitating diseases like malaria, blackwater fever, dysentery, dengue fever and a host of other tropical illnesses taking hold. Add physical exhaustion due to sleep deprivation and an insufficient and irregular diet and you have a recipe for disaster. No Japanese pilot, regardless of his prowess or determination, would be an effective fighter under these horrific conditions.

As previously mentioned in this volume, by mid-August 1943 the offensive that would finally destroy Japanese air power in the Southwest Pacific was about to begin. While the Fifth and Thirteenth Air Forces held a numerical advantage, it was not a great one – at least on paper. Fifth Air Force now had six

One of the last Sentais to fly the Ki-61 was the 55th, whose aircraft are seen here lined up at Sano, in Japan, shortly after the war. Between November 1944 and January 1945 the 55th was assigned to the Philippines, with unfortunate results. On its first sortie in-theater on 24 November the unit had five pilots killed in action, including its CO, Maj Shigeo Iwahashi. (National Museum of the USAF)

squadrons of P-38G/Hs ready for action – the 9th, 39th, 80th, 431st, 432nd and 433rd. This would drop to just five during August when the 39th was forced to replace its worn out Lightnings with P-47Ds, and then four in November when the 9th did the same.

As USAAF and Marine Corps air commanders gathered their forces, the JAAF was concentrating a large force in the Wewak area. There, they constructed four airfields – Hansa, Wewak, But and Aitape. Other major bases in the region includes Hollandia, Lae, Madang and Salamaua. Between August 10 and September 20 there was a constant stream of JAAF units and aircraft making their way from Rabaul into New Guinea. The 68th and 78th Sentais were already at Wewak, and the JAAF had hoped that the new Ki-61 units would be able to counter the strong Allied build up. However, the newness of the Hien was also its Achilles' heel, as it suffered from far too many quality control issues that caused crippling servicing problems.

Those aircraft that did make it aloft suffered terrible losses in the early phase of the offensive, while the unserviceable machines were destroyed in a series of surprise bombing raids generated by information supplied by Allied code breakers. In the days leading up to the offensive they had provided Fifth Air Force mission planners with accurate reports on JAAF units being moved into New Guinea – size, strength and dates were now at hand. Armed with this information Wewak was targeted for attack.

The bombing missions began on August 17 when a force of B-24s attacked at night. With their bases having suffered damaged runways, JAAF units were unable to take-off, and as night turned to day B-25s (escorted by 74 P-38s) came roaring in and destroyed 40 aircraft on the ground, many of them Ki-61s. Not a single Japanese fighter rose to the challenge. This was the first of many devastating raids, with Wewak being bombed numerous times in coming months until all fighter sentai in New Guinea, including both the 68th and 78th, were completely annihilated.

These ex-19th Sentai Ki-61s were captured intact near Manila in early 1945. The frequent failure of Japan to support and maintain its far-flung air assets had a crippling effect on its war effort. As the Allies advanced it was not uncommon to find large numbers of JAAF and IJNAF aircraft intact but grounded due to a lack of spare parts and good maintenance. (National Archives)

STATISTICS AND ANALYSIS

At the beginning of the Pacific War the Allies were just able to hold their own in fighter-versus-fighter combat. As the months passed the Allies began to utilize superior tactics as they quickly embraced new air warfare concepts. While the Japanese favored maneuverability, the Americans believed that speed of escape, ruggedness, firepower, teamwork and high altitude performance were the best ways to fight. And when the P-38 Lightning began to arrive in strength the Japanese had no real answer.

According to Japanese accounts and US statistics, the JAAF lost huge numbers of experienced pilots. Its high command's refusal to rotate groups and squadrons out of the combat zone made it next to impossible for them to reconstitute new units. By the end of 1943 the Allies had achieved an approximate operational superiority of two-to-one or more.

Remarkably, there were never more than 15 squadrons of P-38s in the South and Southwest Pacific at any one time. And when the Fifth Air Force was attacking air bases at Wewak and Rabaul in the summer of 1943, there were just six squadrons of Lightnings in operation. At the same time the JAAF's 4th and 6th Air Armies moved from Rabaul to Wewak. Their maximum strength as of August 15 was estimated to be 250 aircraft. Shortly after this, American attacks on But and Wewak quickly reduced that number, and by the middle of September the JAAF had just over 150 aircraft in-theater. Further reinforcements were flown in but the JAAF would never reach its peak strength again.

The destructive Fifth Air Force attacks forced the JAAF to move its aircraft from Wewak to Hollandia, further up the coast. By April 1944 Hollandia as an air base had been destroyed too, and the JAAF was knocked out of the war as an effective

Maj Ed "Porky" Cragg led the 80th FS from March 1943 until his death in action over Cape Gloucester on Boxing Day 1943. By then his tally stood at 15 victories, including three "Tony" kills. (Rocker via Ethell)

fighting force altogether. Destruction was even more complete here than at Wewak. Technical intelligence identified, by examining engines and fuselage plates, 340 aircraft destroyed on the ground at Hollandia alone.

Even though the enemy's available aircraft strength remained high in 1943-44, the pilot quality was gone. The experienced leaders and crews had been killed and a large percentage of the component technicians and mechanics, of which Japan had only a very limited number, had been overrun in the landings and taken to the hills with no chance of evacuation.

According to Japanese records obtained after the war, by early April 1944 the JAAF had lost more than 95 percent of its experienced pilots who had between 300-600 hours flying time. The overall experience level of the JAAF had been reduced to 30 percent of the level that had existed at the start of the war.

Against the Ki-61, the P-38 was clearly the superior fighter. While postwar JAAF records suggest the Hien may have shot down more Lightnings in New Guinea than both the "Oscar" or the IJNAF's Zero-sen, Lightning pilots were more than happy to meet the "Tony" in combat. Its heavier weight made it less maneuverable, but below 20,000ft the Ki-61 was able to chase a P-38 in level flight or in a dive. While Japanese pilots believed they were shooting down large numbers of P-38s, the reality was very few Lightnings were lost in combat over New Guinea and the Solomons. Indeed, the 475th FG lost just 80 P-38s in action between August 1943 and June 1945.

The highest scoring unit credited with the most Ki-61 victories was the 80th FS with 35. This was followed by the 475th FG's trio of units, who split 46 kills between them, then the 9th FS with 17 confirmed and the 39th with 7. All told, the P-38 units were officially credited with the destruction of 105 "Tonys" in the South and Southwest Pacific. These figures should be taken as estimates, however, as the initial appearance of the new inline-engined fighter led to some hesitant presumptions on the part of intelligence officers. In early reports, the generic term of "fighter" was used to indicate a confirmed victory without specifying "Oscar", "Zeke" or "Tony".

Ranking American ace Capt Dick Bong (40 kills) is seen in conversation with fellow high-scorer Lt Col Tom Lynch (20 kills) at Cape Gloucester in early 1944. Between them they claimed four "Tonys" destroyed. Bong is sitting on his famous P-38J-15 Lightning 42-103993 *Marge*, in which he claimed his last "Tony" on February 15, 1944 for his 22nd kill. Lynch was shot down and killed by flak over Tadji on March 8, 1944. (via John Stanaway)

Cyril F. Homer of the 80th FS was the highest scoring Ki-61 ace with five confirmed. He ended the war as a triple ace, with 15 confirmed victories. The two highest scoring aces of the war, Dick Bong (40 kills) and Tom McGuire (38 kills), who both flew P-38s, ended the war with a total of five "Tonys" between them.

From the Japanese perspective, the air campaign waged in the skies over New Guinea was a complete and catastrophic disaster, with both the 68th and 78th Sentais being totally annihilated in just a matter of months. While almost a dozen Ki-61 pilots achieved ace status in-theater, most did not survive the desperate fighting in the Southwest Pacific. The few that did managed to fight on in the Philippines and later over Japan.

In April 1944 the Americans landed at Hollandia, forcing the 68th Sentai to evacuate. By July both the 68th and 78th had been disbanded. The remaining air and groundcrews joined the infantry or perished in the jungle.

In the end more than 1,800 Japanese aircraft were destroyed by P-38s from the Fifth, Seventh, and Thirteenth Air Forces in the Pacific, and the Tenth and Fourteenth Air Forces in China and Burma. The 475th FG alone accounted for an astonishing 552. Fifth Air Force numbers for enemy aircraft destroyed by both fighter and bomber units from September 1942 through to August 1945 were recorded as 5,594 destroyed, with a further 2,181 as probables and damaged.

The destruction of both JAAF and IJNAF units in the South and Southwest Pacific during 1943-44 ended any hope of Japanese victory. The losses inflicted were too great and the Japanese were never able to recover. While they realized that they could never match America in industrial output, they completely missed the importance of industrial technique.

When comparing the Ki-61 and P-38, it is clear the Japanese were capable of designing a fighter that could match second-generation US machines. But when it came to production, both in terms of numbers and quality, this is where the Japanese failed to meet the standard. They were unable to create complex aviation subsystems that required fine tolerances. Performance and reliability suffered as a result, with the "Tony" being a shining example. Even as the factories began to produce aircraft in greater quantities, the number of fighters in the combat zone did not increase during the first two years of the war. In the end, the Ki-61 Hien would be used in limited numbers in the defense of the Philippines, the Japanese Home Islands, where special ramming units were formed to combat American B-29 attacks and, finally, in supporting the kamikaze attacks off Okinawa and Japan.

For the Americans the Lightning just got better with the introduction of the P-38J/L in 1944. And with enough aircraft for both Europe and the Pacific, more Lightning groups were formed and put to work in the final push towards Japan.

An incredible 100 pilots became aces flying the twin-boomed P-38 in the Pacific and Asia. Its unique qualities of speed, range, firepower, high altitude performance and durability making it the fighter of choice.

Very few Ki-61 pilots survived the air battle over New Guinea, and all operational records of both the 68th and 78th Sentais were destroyed. It must also be noted that claims made by JAAF pilots cannot be taken at face value, and the Japanese had no established rules for determining an aerial victory. They did have gun cameras, but

Cpl Susumu Kajinami poses next to the tail of Ki-27 of the 246th Sentai in Japan in early 1943. One of the few fighter pilots to survive New Guinea, he claimed 23 kills flying the Ki-61 with the 68th Sentai, although this tally is disputed by historians. Kajinami was officially credited with eight victories. (via S Koyama)

Susumu Kajinami was assigned to the 68th Sentai's 2nd Chutai, and he is seen here standing next to a Ki-61 destined for the unit at Kagamihara, Japan, shortly before heading to Wewak in August 1943. Amongst the aircraft claimed destroyed by Kajinami were six P-38s. (via S Koyama)

they were only used for training. The numbers given for Japanese pilots are, for all intents and purposes, unverified claims, and represent a mixture of confirmed, unconfirmed, probable, damaged and imagined victories.

Leading P-38 Lightning Aces of the Fifth Air Force	
Richard Bong	40 (3 "Tonys")
Thomas McGuire	38 (2 "Tonys")
Charles MacDonald	27 (1 "Tony")
Jay Robbins	22 (2 "Tonys")
Gerald Johnson	21 (2 "Tonys", + 1 in P-47D – 22 final score)
Thomas Lynch	17 (1 "Tony", + 3 in P-400 – 20 final score)
Edward Cragg	15 (3 "Tonys")
Cyril Homer	15 (5 "Tonys")
Daniel Roberts	13 (0 "Tonys", + 2 in P-400 – 15 final score)
Robert Westbrook	13 (0 "Tonys", + 7 in P-40F – 20 final score)
Kenneth Ladd	12 (0 "Tonys")
Cornelius Smith	11 (1 "Tony")
James Watkins	11 (5 "Tonys", + 1 in P-40E – 12 final score)
Fred Champlin	9 (0 "Tonys")
Meryl Smith	9 (1 "Tony")
George Welch	9 (3 "Tonys", + 4 in P-40B and 3 in P-39D – 16 final score)
Kenneth Hart	8 (2 "Tonys")
John O'Neill	8 (0 "Tonys")
Richard West	8 (1 "Tony", + 6 in P-40N – 14 final score)
Robert Aschenbrener	7 (5 "Tonys", + 3 in P-40N – 10 final score)
Richard Smith	7 (2 "Tonys")
Burt Adams	6 (1 "Tony", + 1 in P-70 – 7 final score)
Stan Andrews	6 (1 "Tony")
Edwin DeGraffenreid	6 (1 "Tony")
Paul Lucas	6 (2 "Tonys")
John Smith	6 (0 "Tonys')

Leading Ki-61 Hien Pilots in New Guinea	
Susumu Kajinami (68th Sentai)	Claimed 24 (including 6 P-38s), official score 8
Shogo Takeuchi (68th Sentai)	Claimed 16 and 10 probables, official score 30+
Takashi Tomishima (78th Sentai)	Claimed 4 (all P-38s), official score 4

AFTERMATH

The P-38 ended the war in the Pacific with an exceptional record. It was the most successful twin-engined fighter of the war. No other single-seat twin-engined aircraft came even close to its performance and exploits. Fittingly, the first USAAF aircraft to land on Japanese soil was a P-38, albeit by accident. While flying a fighter patrol on August 16, 1945, Lt Col Clay Tice Jr and Flt Off Douglas Hall of the 49th FG found themselves short on fuel and were forced to land.

The Supreme Allied Commander in the Pacific, Gen Douglas MacArthur, subsequently selected the 49th FG to be the first fighter unit assigned to Japan.

Providing high cover, Lightnings of the 49th FG escort Japanese surrender envoys as they approach Ie Shima on their way to Manila, in the Philippines. The white-painted G4M "Bettys" are accompanied by a B-25 Mitchell from the 499th BS and a B-17H Air-Sea Rescue aircraft carrying an airborne lifeboat. (*National Archives*)

On September 8 the group flew to Atsugi air base, on Honshu, and became the occupational fighter force. The 49th would later trade its P-38Ls for P-51Ds in December. Lightnings of the 49th also had the honor of escorting the Japanese surrender party as it flew from Japan to the airfield on the island of le Shima on August 19, 1945.

After the war the P-38 remained in service until 1949. Those left behind in the Pacific were burned or bulldozed into the ground. Postwar, 50 P-38s were sold to Italy's emerging air force and 12 were given to Honduras. In the end Lightnings completed 130,000 combat missions and equipped 27 fighter groups and ten photo-reconnaissance groups. All told, 10,037 were produced.

Sadly, the aircraft's two highest scoring aces did not survive the war, Dick Bong being killed while test flying Lockheed's newest jet fighter, the P-80 Shooting Star, on August 6, 1945, and Tommy McGuire crashing to his death while trying to maneuver behind a lone Ki-43 just above the trees on January 7, 1945. With its long-range tanks still attached, his P-38 snap-rolled and plunged into the jungle.

In the closing months of the war, the Ki-61 became a symbol of Japan's defense against the high-flying USAAF B-29s. The "Tony" was one of the few single-seat fighters capable of reaching the Superfortresses at altitude. But like the battles in the Southwest Pacific, the Ki-61 units assigned to home defense never really had a telling effect. In desperation, like their IJNAF counterparts, the JAAF pilots resorted to suicidal ramming tactics.

In January 1945 the USAAF destroyed the Akashi engine plant responsible for the Ki-61's Ha-40 and the new Ha-140 powerplants. With no new engines, and 275 engineless Ki-61-II airframes, the Japanese quickly married the Mitsubishi Ha-112H radial engine to the proven Ki-61. The new machine, the Ki-100, was arguably one of the best Japanese single-seat fighters of the war. For the first time the Ki-61 airframe

Maj Tom McGuire pushed Bong hard for the title of "ace of aces", being killed in action 12 days after claiming his 38th victory. Seen here in his P-38L-1 *PUDGY (V)*, McGuire claimed two "Tonys" destroyed. (via John Stanaway)

had a dependable engine rated at 1,500hp. Its speed was slightly slower, but it was lighter, with a better rate of climb and improved maneuverability at higher altitudes. By the end of May 1945 all 275 of the otherwise useless airframes had been converted into Ki-100s. But it was far too late, and the Ki-100 had no impact whatsoever.

The last major combat between the JAAF and American fighter units occurred on July 25, 1945, when 18 Ki-100s of the 244th Sentai clashed with ten F6F-5 Hellcats of VF-31 over Yokaichi airfield. In the short, sharp action the 244th claimed 12 Hellcats destroyed for the loss of two pilots. On the American side the US Navy pilots claimed eight kills (four aircraft identified as "Franks" were shot down by Lt C. N. Noy) for no loss.

After the war, countries formerly occupied by the Japanese were quick to rebuild their air forces with the hundreds of abandoned aircraft left behind by the JAAF. According to the *US Strategic Bombing Survey*, titled "Japanese Air Power", there were 1,000 Japanese aircraft remaining in Southeast Asia in various states of repair. There were also unspecified numbers in China, Manchuria, Korea and other Japanese outposts that were not reported. Many of these aircraft were unserviceable, and would remain that way due to the lack of spare parts and trained groundcrews. In the case of China both the Communists and Nationalists had access to a large variety of Japanese military aircraft, including the Ki-61. The remaining "Tonys" were duly pressed into service, but the Chinese had even less success with the aircraft than the Japanese due to chronic engine problems and a lack of spare parts.

The results achieved by the Allied air forces in the air battles above New Guinea and the Solomons were remarkable. The sheer physical damage suffered by both the JAAF and IJNAF was staggering, and one from which they would not recover. The role played by the P-38 cannot be understated. In the tough years of 1943 and early 1944, the small numbers available took the fight to the enemy and contributed greatly to the final victory.

Once a foe, now a friend. This hastily painted Ki-61 bears the markings of the Nationalist Chinese air force. It would change hands one more time when the Chinese Communists captured Peiping from the Nationalists in November 1945. (National Museum of the USAF)

FURTHER READING

BOOKS

Bergerud, Eric M., *Fire In the Sky* (Westview Press, 2001)

Bodie, Warren M. and Jeffrey Ethell, *World War II Pacific War Eagles in Original Color* (Widewing Publications, 1997)

Bueschel, Richard M., *Kawasaki Ki-61 Hien in Japanese Army Air Force Service* (Schiffer Publishing, 1996)

Caidin, Martin, *Zero Fighter* (Ballantine Books Inc., 1971)

Caidin, Martin, *Fork-Tailed Devil: The P-38* (Ballantine Books Inc., 1973)

Davis, Larry, *P-38 in Action* (Squadron/Signal Publications, 1983)

Ethell, Jeffrey L. et al. *Great Book of World War II Airplanes. Twelve Volumes.* (Bonanza Books, 1984)

Francillon, Rene J., *Japanese Aircraft of the Pacific War* (Naval Institute Press, 1994)

Green, William, *Fighters Volume Three* (Macdonald & Co Ltd, 1961)

Hata, Ikuhiko, Izawa, Yasuho and Christopher Shores, *Japanese Army Air Force Fighter Units and their Aces 1931-1945* (Grub Street 2002)

Hees, William N., *Osprey Elite Units 14 – 49th Fighter Group* (Osprey Publishing, 2004)

Holmes, Tony, *Osprey Aircraft of the Aces 61 – 'Twelve to One' - V Fighter Command Aces of the Pacific War* (Osprey Publishing, 2004)

Jarrett, Philip, *Aircraft of the Second World War* (Putnam 1997)

Mikesh, Robert C., *Broken Wing of the Samurai – The Destruction of the Japanese Air Force* (Airlife, 1993)

Nijboer, Donald, *Graphic War – The Secret Aviation Drawings and Illustrations of World War II* (Boston Mills Press, 2005)

Nijboer, Donald, *Cockpit: An Illustrated History* (Boston Mills Press, 1998)
Okumiya, Masatake, Horikoshi, Jiro and Martin Caidin, *Zero* (Ballantine Books, 1973)
O'Leary, Michael, *Osprey Production Line to Frontline 3 – Lockheed P-38 Lightning* (Osprey Publishing, 1999)
Price, Alfred, *Fighter Aircraft* (Arms & Armour Press, 1989)
Sakai, Saburo, *Samurai* (Ballantine Books, 1963)
Sakaida, Henry, *Osprey Aircraft of the Aces 13 – Japanese Army Air Force Aces 1937-45* (Osprey Publishing, 1997)
Stanaway, John, *Osprey Aircraft of the Aces 14 – P-38 Lightning Aces of the Pacific and CBI* (Osprey Publishing, 1997)
Stanaway, John, *Osprey Aviation Elite Units 23 – 475th Fighter Group* (Osprey Publishing, 2007)

MAGAZINE ARTICLES

Meyer, Corky, "1944 Fighter Conference", *Flight Journal Special World War II Fighters* (February 2001)
O'Leary, Michael, "Database Lockheed P-38 Lightning", *Aeroplane Monthly* (February 2003)
Picarella, Giuseppe, "Under New Management", *Aeroplane Monthly* (May 2007)
Picarella, Giuseppe, "Uncle Sam's Swallows", *Aeroplane Monthly* (October 2008)

WEBSITES

Acepilots.com
Flyingknights.net
j-aircraft.com
475thfghf.org

INDEX

References to illustrations are shown in **bold**.